Gamedev Production and Design Workbook

Practical Companion for Producers, Designers & Leads

A hybrid guide-and-notebook for structuring your game projects, meetings, and production workflows.

by Leszek Lisowski

First Edition
ISBN: 978-83-976281-2-0

This workbook is a practical tool. Use the templates as inspiration and adapt them to your personal processes.

https://leszeklisowski.com

Dedication

I've been making games for about twenty years now. Long enough to know two things:

1. this work is never really "done", and
2. I still reach for a pen when things get messy.

I made this workbook because I like - and need - to write things down. Every time I opened a digital notes app, I ended up back on paper anyway. At the same time, I kept wishing I had a small, practical set of reminders and frameworks within arm's reach - even if some of them are "obvious" once you see them.

Game development has a talent for forcing us to rediscover the same lessons over and over. My hope is that this little collection of those lessons can save you a bit of time, a bit of frustration, and maybe one or two avoidable disasters.

This workbook is for you if...

- You work on games with more than just your keyboard - as a producer, designer, lead, or anyone who keeps projects moving.
- You're constantly juggling meetings, builds, features, and feedback, and you want one physical place that connects it all.
- Blank notebooks annoy you: you prefer light structure and prompts instead of 200 empty pages.
- You like writing by hand, but you also want the page next to your notes to actually help you think.
- You sometimes catch yourself "rediscovering" the same production or design lesson and would rather have it written down once.
- You've been in game dev for years or you're just starting out, but you already know this: shipping games is hard, and any honest, practical help is welcome.

How to Use This Workbook

I designed this workbook as something I needed myself: a place where I write on the right page like I always do, and still have useful game dev reminders on the left instead of empty paper or random screenshots.
The idea is simple:

- left page = a small framework, checklist, or reminder from real game development,
- right page = your world: your project, your meetings, your ideas, your mess.

Nothing here is a strict rule. Everything on this page is a suggestion. It's your workbook, your work, your projects. Use whatever helps and ignore the rest.
Some pages will feel obvious. That's fine. In the middle of production chaos, even "obvious" things are easy to forget. The left side is there to nudge you; the right side is where you make it real.

Page layout at a glance

On each left page you might find:

- **Title** – what this page focuses on (for example: „Milestone Definition", „Core Loop", „Playtest Scenario").
- **Short context** – 1–2 sentences: why this matters in real projects.
- **Framework / Cheatsheet** – a compact list, grid or steps you can glance at during a meeting or planning session.
- **Try this** – a few prompts to help you apply the idea to your current game.
- **Watch out** – common mistakes and traps related to this topic.

On each right page you'll usually have:

- A small space at the top for date, project / game name, meeting / sprint / topic.
- A free place for free notes, sketches, lists, flows, or whatever you need on paper.
- Icon & block – a small icon telling you which area this page belongs to
- (foundations, planning, production, design, business, team, personal workflow).

I personally treat the left page as a mini tool, and the right page as the place where real work happens.

Ways to use it

Use this workbook in whatever way actually helps you. A few examples:

- **One pair of pages per meeting** – pick a left page that fits (planning, production, team), take all your meeting notes on the right.
- **One pair per feature or problem** – use the left page as a thinking frame (scope, risks, design), break everything down on the right.
- **Review & retro support** – open a page from production or team blocks to structure your thoughts, capture outcomes on the right.
- **Personal planning** – use the „personal workflow" pages as a quick weekly plan, then fill the right side with tasks and follow-ups.
- **Scratchpad** – if none of the left pages match what you're doing, ignore them and just use the right side for raw notes and doodles.

You don't have to use pages in order. Jump around. Repeat a topic. Reuse the same kind of page for different projects. Mix structured notes with messy scribbles.

There is no wrong way to use this workbook. It's a tool to help you ship games a bit more consciously – whether you're capturing meeting notes, rough ideas for new features, next actions for your team, or simply doodling in the margins to clear your head.

Find the Right Page for Your Situation

This page is here for the moments when you don't have time to browse the whole notebook.
Scan the situations on the left, pick the one that's closest to what you're dealing with right now in your game, and jump to the suggested blocks on the right.

Use this as a starting point, not a rulebook – if another block fits better, use that instead. If you got your idea or vision that fits your needs better – go ahead.

Situation / Need	Where to go (blocks)
You're defining a new game or resetting the vision for an existing one.	**Foundations & Vision** – pages on vision, pillars, target audience, success metrics.
You're preparing for a milestone or greenlight review of your game.	**Planning & Scoping + Production & Processes** – milestones, scope, risks, build checks.
You're about to run sprint planning or iteration planning for your team.	**Planning & Scoping + Production & Processes** – roadmap, sprint basics, backlog, dependencies.
You need to break down features, cut scope, or make hard trade-offs.	**Planning & Scoping** – feature breakdown, prioritisation, cutting features, buffers and constraints.
You're working on your game's core loop, progression, or economy.	**Game Design & UX** – core loop, meta progression, economy basics, player journey.
You're planning or running a playtest or review session for your game.	**Game Design & UX** + Production & Processes – playtest scenarios, evaluation, retros and postmortems.
You're planning a launch, update, or important store page changes.	**Business, Store & Marketing** – store checklists, launch readiness, post-launch focus, messaging.
You're dealing with team communication, stakeholders, or tension in the group.	**Team & Communication** – meetings, 1:1s, feedback, decision log, conflict basics, stakeholder map.
You want to get your own work under control and protect your focus.	**Personal Workflow & Growth** – daily/weekly planning, priority matrix, deep work, boundaries, burnout signals.

Blocks Overview – What the Icons Mean

Every left page in this workbook belongs to one of the blocks below.
The small icon in the corner of the right page tells you which part of game development these pages focus on.
Use this legend when you want to quickly jump to the kind of help you need right now.

Foundations & Vision 🧭 (compass)
Big-picture thinking for your game: vision, pillars, target audience, constraints, success metrics.
Use these pages when you're defining a new game, resetting direction, or checking if everyone still shares the same vision.

Planning & Scoping 📅 (calendar page)
Roadmaps, milestones, scope, prioritisation, buffers, vertical slices, change requests.
Use these pages when you're planning what to build next, preparing a milestone, or deciding what to cut and what to keep.

Production & Processes ⚙ (gear)
Daily production reality: sprints, boards, builds, bug triage, pipelines, freezes, retros, incident reviews.
Use these pages when you're in the middle of production and need to keep things moving without losing control.

Game Design & UX 🎮 (controller)
Core loop, progression, economy, onboarding, difficulty, level flow, playtests and evaluation.
Use these pages when you're shaping how your game actually plays and feels for the player.

Business, Store & Marketing 📈 (chart)
Store pages, launch planning, post-launch focus, monetisation models, messaging, community and reviews.
Use these pages when you're preparing a launch, updating store assets, or thinking about how your game reaches players.

Team & Communication 👥 (silhouettes)
Meetings, 1:1s, feedback, stakeholders, decisions, conflicts, handoffs, basic hiring and onboarding notes.
Use these pages when you're dealing with people: aligning the team, handling tensions, or making and recording decisions.

Personal Workflow & Growth 🕒 (clock)
Your own way of working: daily and weekly planning, priorities, focus time, boundaries, burnout signals, learning goals.
Use these pages when you want to get your own work under control, protect your focus, or plan how you grow in game dev.

My Current Project

Game title:

Genre:

Platforms:

My role:

Target audience:

One-sentence vision for this game:

Short description of the game:

Main goals for this game in the next months:

Notes I want to remember about this game:

Block A
Foundations & Vision

Topic: .... Date: ....

Producer / Designer: The Real Job

Job titles look nice on LinkedIn. Games don't ship because of job titles.
Your real role is defined by what you actually take responsibility for when things get messy.
This page is here to strip your role down to what matters: what you own, what you enable, and what you should probably stop doing.

Producer – in practice

As a producer, you typically:

- Keep the roadmap and reality in sync – what we want vs what we can actually do.
- Make sure people know what to work on next and why it matters.
- Clarify scope and priorities before work hits art/code/audio.
- Track builds, blockers and risks and push to get them unblocked.
- Connect disciplines (design, art, code, QA, marketing) so information flows both ways.
- Protect time and focus where it matters most – especially around milestones.
- Drive decisions and follow-ups after meetings instead of letting them evaporate.

You're not "the boss of everyone". You're the person who keeps the project moving and coherent.

Designer – in practice

As a designer, you typically:

- Own how the game plays and feels – core loop, systems, pacing, moment-to-moment.
- Turn vague ideas into clear, testable specs that other people can actually build.
- Think about the player's experience, not just the feature list.
- Work with art, code and audio so the design survives contact with reality.
- Iterate on paper, prototypes and builds, not only in documents.
- Keep an eye on difficulty, onboarding and usability as the game grows.
- Use feedback and data to adjust, simplify or kill features when needed.

You're not just writing docs. You're responsible for making sure the game is playable, understandable and worth playing.

Where you overlap

Producers and designers are different roles, but good ones share a few habits:

- Both care about the player first, not their own spreadsheet or document.
- Both show up for playtests and reviews, and treat feedback seriously.
- Both help the team make and record decisions, instead of leaving everything "open".
- Both communicate clearly and early when something is off – scope, quality, or vision.

If either role hides in their tools (Jira, Miro, Notion, whatever) and avoids the game and the team, the project suffers.

Try this

- On the right page, write this down for your current game:
- Three things I am truly responsible for in this project (things that break if I stop doing them):
- Three things I'm doing that I probably shouldn't (busywork, rescuing others, filling gaps that should be solved differently):
- One change I want to make in how I show up in this role in the next weeks:

Watch out for

- Acting like a firewall instead of a bridge – blocking information instead of connecting people.
- Swinging between no decisions at all and micromanaging every detail.
- "Designing" or "producing" only inside tools (Excel, Miro, Jira) and not spending enough time with the actual game build and the people making it.

This page is a mirror. Use it to be honest about what your job really is on this game – and what you want it to be.

Topic: .... Date: ....

Game Vision One-Pager

A vision is not a 40-page GDD. It's a simple, shared picture of what you're trying to build and why it's worth finishing. It should be short enough for people to remember it, and clear enough to guide real decisions: what you say yes to, what you say no to, and what you cut when time runs out.
Use this one-pager as a filter for your game, not as marketing copy. If a feature, idea or request doesn't fit this page, it's a good candidate to drop, park, or rethink.

The one-page vision structure

Title / Working title
The name you actually use when you talk about the game today. If the real name is still in flux, write the working title you're using with the team.

High concept
One or two sentences that answer: What is this game?
Think in terms of genre and core activity, not tech.
Example pattern:
"[Game] is a [genre] game about [core activity] for [target player]."

Core fantasy / player promise
What fantasy are you delivering when someone plays this?
What do they get to be or feel that they don't get in real life?
Keep it concrete: "feeling like a...", "solving...", "surviving...", not just "having fun".

Target player
Who is this really for?
Short description: typical age/experience level, what they usually play, how they usually play (short sessions, long marathons, chill after work, competitive evenings etc.).
Avoid "everyone". Think of a real person you know.

Platforms & scope level
Which platforms you are actually aiming for, and roughly how big this game is meant to be.
Small / mid / big in your own context – a focused, 5–10 hour experience is a very different beast than a 200-hour sandbox.
This line should match your constraints and team, not your dreams.

Key references
List a few games that are meaningful references for you: where you sit on the "X meets Y" axis.
You can also note what you're taking from each reference (tone, structure, controls, economy depth, etc.), not just the names.

"Success looks like..." (teaser)
A short, rough note on what success means for this game: for you, your team, and your players.
You'll refine this later using the Success Metrics page – here, a few simple phrases are enough to capture the direction.

Try this

- Do a quick, rough pass of the one-pager for your current game on the right page.

Don't polish wording, don't wordsmith. Aim for clarity, not cleverness.

- If you get stuck on a field, write the simplest honest version you can and move on. You can always refine later.
- When you're done, ask yourself:

"If the whole team had this in front of them, would it change how we decide what to do next?"

Watch out for

- Turning this into another long document – if it doesn't fit on a single page, you're writing too much.
- Writing marketing slogans instead of a clear internal vision. This page is for the team first, not for the store page.
- Avoiding hard choices by staying vague – a useful vision also says what this game is not.
- Letting the one-pager rot while the project changes. When the game shifts, either update the vision or admit you're now building a different game.

Topic: .... Date: ....

High Concept & Elevator Pitch That People Actually Understand

If your pitch only makes sense to people already inside the project, it's not doing its job.
A high concept and a short elevator pitch should let someone outside the team understand, in plain language, what your game is and why it's worth caring about.
The high concept is the skeleton: clear, compact, reusable.
The elevator pitch adds a bit of flesh: a few sentences that make someone want to hear more.

High concept – the core sentence

Your high concept answers, in one breath:
What is this game, about what, and for whom?
Use a simple pattern like:
"[Game] is a [genre] game about [core activity] for [target player]."
You can extend it with references if it genuinely helps:
"[Game] is a [genre] game about [core activity] for [target player], inspired by [references]."
Guidelines:

- Focus on genre + core activity + player, not technology.
- Use plain words your team, publisher and players all understand.
- If you need more than 1–2 sentences, you're slipping into description, not high concept.

Elevator pitch – 2–3 sentences that land

An elevator pitch is what you say when someone asks:
"So, what's your game?"
In 2–3 sentences, it should:

1. Say what the game is (high concept, simplified).
2. Say what the player does and feels.
3. Hint at what makes it different from other games in that space.

For example, structure it like this:

1. Sentence 1 – high concept in human words.
2. Sentence 2 – what the player actually does moment to moment.
3. Sentence 3 – 1–2 clear things that make it stand out.

You can (and should) tune the wording depending on who you talk to:

- For a developer – slightly more concrete about systems and scope.
- For a publisher – clearer about target player, market slot and risk.
- For a player – focused on fantasy, feeling and what they actually get to do.

These versions should feel like the same game, just told in different language – not three completely different pitches.

Try this
On the right page, draft:

- One high concept sentence using the template:

"[Game] is a [genre] game about [core activity] for [target player]."

- Three elevator pitch variants for the same game:
  - one for a developer,
  - one for a publisher,
  - one for a player.
- For each version, underline the parts that change.
- Check: are you changing mainly the language and focus, not the actual game?

If you can't say your pitch out loud in under 20–30 seconds without stumbling, simplify it and try again.

Watch out for

- Talking about technology instead of the player: engines, shaders and pipelines don't belong in your pitch.
- Hiding behind buzzwords: if your pitch uses "immersive", "innovative" or "deep gameplay", rewrite it.
- Filling the pitch with genre clichés and nothing specific to your game.
- Letting different team members use completely different descriptions – that's a sign your vision isn't aligned yet.

Topic: .... Date: ....

Game Pillars That Actually Help

Pillars are not slogans for a slide.
Good pillars are simple rules that help your team say yes or no to real decisions.
If a "pillar" doesn't change how you handle a feature, level, asset, or request, it's just noise. A small set of strong pillars keeps your game recognisable and protects it when time and pressure hit.
Aim for a few pillars you can actually remember. Four is often a sweet spot – stable like a table – but the number matters less than how useful they are.

What a good pillar looks like

A good game pillar should:

- Describe how this game should feel or behave, not just its genre.
- Be specific enough to rule some ideas out.
- Be short – one short label + one clear sentence.
- Come with at least one concrete example decision it will guide.

Quick examples:
Good pillar (clear and useful)

- "Readable, low-friction controls for tired evening players."
- "Every run must create at least one meaningful, memorable choice."
- "Short, self-contained sessions that feel complete in under 25 minutes."

Vague pillar (slogan, not a tool)

- "Fun and engaging gameplay."
- "Immersive experience."
- "Deep and replayable."

If you can't imagine a real situation where a pillar helps you pick one option over another, it's not doing its job.

Simple template for your pillars
For each pillar, you want three things:

1. Name – a short label people can repeat.
2. Explanation (1 sentence) – what this means in practice.
3. Example decision – one real-world decision this pillar helps you make.

Structure it like this:

- Pillar name – one short phrase.
- This means: one clear sentence.
- This helps us decide: one example:
- "We choose A over B because it fits this pillar better."

On the right page, you can draft your own set of pillars using this pattern.

Try this
On the right page, write down your pillars for the game you're working on now:

1. Draft 3–4 pillars using the template above.
2. For each pillar, add at least one concrete decision it should influence, e.g.:
   - cut / keep a feature,
   - accept / reject an asset,
   - change / keep a mechanic as it is.
3. Read them out loud as if you were explaining them to a new team member. If they sound like corporate fluff, rewrite until they're clear and grounded.

You know you're done when you can take a random idea and honestly say:
"According to our pillars, this fits" or "According to our pillars, this should go."

Watch out for

- Pillars that describe everything and nothing: "fun", "innovative", "high quality".
- Pillars that just repeat the genre: "this is an FPS", "this is a cozy game" – that's not guidance.
- Writing pillars and then ignoring them the moment a shiny idea appears.
- Adding more and more pillars until no one can remember or use them.

Pillars are only useful if they shape real decisions. If they don't change anything you do, you don't need them.

Topic: .... Date: ....

Target Player Snapshot

You are not building this game for a vague blob called "everyone", but for specific people, with specific lives, habits and limits.

A good target player snapshot combines two things:

- who they are (age range, experience, basic demographics), and
- how they live and play (time, energy, platform, headspace).

This is not a marketing persona slide to impress someone in a deck. It's a quick, practical picture that should change how you design, scope and prioritise.

What goes into a useful snapshot

Keep it short and concrete. On the right page, aim to capture:

Age range & experience

- Rough age band (e.g. "late 20s–mid 30s", "teenage", "40+"),
- How experienced they are with this genre and platform (new, mid-core, very experienced).

Context of play

- When they usually play (evenings after work/school, weekends, commute, late-night sessions),
- How long typical sessions are,
- What state they're in when they start playing (tired, stressed, relaxed, competitive mood, etc.).

Platform & hardware

- Primary platform for this game (PC, console, mobile, handheld),
- Any relevant hardware constraints (old laptop, shared console, gamepad vs mouse/keyboard, touch only).

What they like and avoid

- Types of games or features they are drawn to (systems, story, chill vibes, challenge, social play, etc.),
- Things that turn them off (long unskippable scenes, high pressure, steep learning curve, grind, FOMO, etc.).

Why they would play this game

- One or two clear reasons they'd pick your game over doing something else with their limited time,
- What they hope to get out of it: feeling, escape, mastery, laughter, competition, calm, etc.

If your snapshot doesn't help you answer "would this person actually enjoy this feature or pacing?", it's not specific enough.

Try this

On the right page, sketch one main target player for your current game:

- Give them an age range and a short label ("tired strategy fan after work", "competitive teen shooter player", etc.).
- Describe in a few lines when and how they play, and on what device.
- List 3 things they generally enjoy in games, and 3 things that usually annoy them.
- Finish with one sentence starting with:
- "They would choose this game when..."

Then, add a small note for yourself:
"This game is primarily for them, not for me."
Use that line as a reminder when your personal taste drifts too far from what this player actually needs.

Watch out for

- Writing "everyone" or "players 18–45" and pretending that's a target.
- Designing mainly for yourself just because you happen to work on the game.
- Stopping at demographics ("male 25–34") with no link to concrete design decisions.
- Treating this as a one-off exercise that never gets updated while the game and audience assumptions change.

A clear target player snapshot should make some ideas obviously stronger and some obviously weaker. If nothing changes in your decisions after writing it, go back and make it sharper.

Topic: .... Date: ....

Genre & Market Positioning

Genre is a shortcut in the player's and store's head: it tells them roughly what to expect before they ever see your game running.
Market positioning is where you decide to sit inside that space – who you stand next to, and what makes you different enough to be noticed. If your competition is "every game in the genre", you don't have a position yet. You need a small, clear neighbourhood and a few conscious differences.

Map your neighbourhood

Think of your game on a simple two-axis map:

- **Horizontal – "Who are we close to?"**

Games that sit near you in genre, camera, platform and audience.
These are the titles your players would also consider buying/playing.

- **Vertical – "How are we different?"**

Axes where you want to stand out, such as:
Fantasy / theme (what the game is about), Core mechanics (what you do most of the time), Tone (serious / silly / chill / intense), Depth & complexity, Session length and pacing, Difficulty and punishment level.

You can also keep in mind platform and business model:
Does your game make sense as a premium title / DLC-driven / F2P within this neighbourhood and for this audience?
If everything about your design screams "short, focused premium experience", forcing it into a grindy live-service model is asking for trouble.
Your goal is to know:

- "We are close to these 3–5 games,"
- "...and we are deliberately different in these specific ways."

Questions to answer for your game
Use the right page to answer, in your own words:

1. **Which games are our closest neighbours?**
   - A short list (3–5 titles) that share genre, perspective, target player and rough scope.
   - These should be games your realistic target player already knows or might discover.
2. **What are we consciously doing differently?**
3. **In concrete terms, not slogans. For example:**
   - Different fantasy or role for the player,
   - Different pacing and session structure,
   - Different focus of depth (fewer systems, but pushed further; or the opposite),
   - Different tone or emotional target.
4. **Does our platform and model fit this picture?**
   - Are we targeting the same kind of device and session pattern as our neighbours?
   - Is our chosen business model something this audience is already comfortable with for this kind of game?

If the answer to "who else is like us?" or "how are we different?" is fuzzy, your positioning isn't ready yet.

Try this
On the right page, sketch a simple map for your current game:

- List 3–5 real games that feel like your closest neighbours.
- For each, write one line: "Close because..." (camera, structure, audience, etc.).
- Then write 3 specific ways your game should be different on purpose.
- Finally, note your platform + business model and ask yourself:

"Would a player who likes those neighbours find this combination natural?"
If you can't explain your differences in a couple of clear sentences, simplify and sharpen until you can.

Watch out for

- Treating "everyone in the genre" as your competition – that's too broad to guide design or marketing.
- Trying so hard to be "unique" that the game stops being readable as part of any genre at all.
- Blindly copying hit games without understanding why they worked for their audience, platform and model.
- Ignoring the fit between your design and your monetisation model – premium-feeling games with tacked-on F2P loops, or F2P structures on players who expect a clean, paid experience.

Clear genre and market positioning should make some decisions easier and some ideas clearly out of bounds. If nothing changes in what you plan to build after writing it down, your positioning isn't concrete enough yet.

Topic: .... Date: ....

What Makes This Game Worth Playing

A USP is not a fancy label or a feature list.
Your unique selling proposition is a clear promise to the player: why they should choose this game instead of doing something else with their time.
If your USP is just "we have these features too", it's not a USP.
If you can't feel it quickly when you actually play, it's probably not real.

What a strong USP really is

A useful USP should:

- Focus on the player's benefit and experience, not only on mechanics.
- Be specific enough that not every game in the genre could claim the same thing.
- Be visible early in gameplay, not only after 10 hours "once it opens up".
- Be something you can support with production – scope, budget, team, tech.

Think of it as the answer to:
"For this kind of player, what do we genuinely do better or differently than others in this space?"
Not more features. Not more hours. A sharper promise.

Two simple USP patterns
You can use patterns like these to draft your USP:

- Player-focused pattern

"Players who enjoy [X] will get [Y unique benefit] from this game because [reason]."

- Genre-focused pattern

"Among [genre] games, this one stands out by [clear difference] for players who [target player]."
Use them as scaffolding, not as final marketing text. The goal is clarity inside the team first.
A good USP should immediately suggest which ideas naturally fit your game – and which don't.

Bad USP patterns to avoid
If your USP sounds like any of these, it's not unique and probably not useful:
"Immersive and engaging gameplay.", "Deep and replayable experience.", "Fun for everyone.", "Next-gen graphics and innovative mechanics.", "Best-in-class gameplay and stunning visuals."
Any decent game could write the same lines. That means they don't help you decide anything.

Try this
On the right page, work through your game's USP:

1. Draft three versions of your USP, using the patterns above.
   - At least one version should be max one sentence.
   - In each version, clearly mark:
     - the player type you're talking about,
     - the benefit/experience they get,
     - the reason your game can deliver it.
2. Ask yourself for each version:
   - "Would a stranger understand why they might choose this game over similar ones?"
   - "Can we show this difference quickly in real gameplay, not only in a pitch deck?"
3. Make a quick feature check:
   - List 3–5 features or ideas from your current design.
   - For each, mark if it strongly supports your USP, weakly supports it, or doesn't support it at all.
   - Anything that doesn't support your USP is first in line when you need to cut or simplify.

Your USP is not just for marketing. It's a knife for cutting scope.

Watch out for

- Confusing "USP" with a single technical feature ("we use this engine / this tech"), instead of the player's experience.
- Promising something your team and budget cannot realistically deliver.
- USP that only exists in trailers and store copy, but not in the actual game.
- Trying to have four different USPs – if everything is "unique", nothing is.
- Quietly changing what makes the game special halfway through production, without updating design and marketing.

A good USP is a commitment:
"This is what we want players to feel, and we're willing to say no to things that don't support it."

Topic: .... Date: ....

Project Constraints: Your Real Box

You never make a game in a vacuum. You always make it inside a box: time, money, people, technology, external commitments.
If you pretend you have no constraints, you're lying to yourself and to your team.
The point is not to complain about the box. The point is to draw its shape clearly, so you can make honest decisions inside it. As a producer (or anyone leading a project), owning this box is part of your job.
Scope that ignores your constraints is fantasy, not a plan.

The main types of constraints

You don't need a perfect list – just a clear one. Most projects have some mix of:

- Time – dates you can't move easily (funding milestones, partner deadlines, holidays, certification windows).
- Budget – money for people, tools, outsourcing, marketing; how long you can realistically keep the team on this game.
- Team – how many people you really have, what they can actually do, seniority, availability, vacations, multi-project load, energy levels.
- Technology – engine, tools, platforms, pipeline, build times, technical debt you're carrying.
- External – licenses, IP owners, publishers, platform rules, legal/regulatory stuff, any stakeholder who can say "no".

Some of these are genuinely hard limits. Others are just "how we've always done it" or "what someone once said".

Your job is to be honest about which is which.

A simple way to write your box

For each category, write one or two short lines:

- What is the constraint?

("We must ship before [event]", "We have no full-time UI artist", "We are locked to this engine version".)

- How does it actually affect this game?

("We can't add a full new mode", "We must keep content modular", "We can't afford long cert cycles".)

Then add a small note:

- Hard or flexible?

Is this really non-negotiable, or could it move if you had a serious discussion with the right person?

Being honest here can be uncomfortable. Sometimes it means admitting you're over-promising or that you need to push back on a boss or partner. It's still better than silently pretending everything fits.

Try this

Use this page to spell out constraints for your current game:

- Write what you know for sure about time, budget, team, tech, external.
- Mark which constraints are truly hard and which you suspect are more flexible than people admit.
- Next to each constraint, note one thing it forces you to do (or not do) in design and production.

Ask yourself:

- "If we respect this box, what must we cut, simplify or delay?"
- "If we ignore this box, where and when will the pain show up – and for whom?"

It's better to have one honest painful conversation now than three crises later.

Watch out for

- Saying "we have no constraints" – you do, even if no one wrote them down yet.
- Treating every constraint as equally hard, so nothing can ever move.
- Pretending the team is an infinite resource – ignoring burnout, context switching, and people already spread across multiple projects.
- Never revisiting constraints after big changes in scope, budget or timeline.

Clear constraints don't kill creativity. They focus it where it actually has a chance to ship.

Topic: ....   Date: ....

Top Risks at the Start of Your Game

The risks exist whether you write them down or not.
The only real choice is: deal with them early, or deal with them later when they're bigger and more expensive.
This page is here to force an honest look at what can go wrong in your game – not just in code, but in product, people, scope and timing. If you lead or produce the project, owning this list is part of your job.
Naming risks will not "jinx" the project. Hiding them will.

The main risk areas

Most game projects carry some mix of risks in a few simple buckets:

- Product / Market – will anyone actually want this game at this time, at this price, on this platform?
- Technology – can your team and tools realistically deliver what you're planning?
- Content – can you create enough content, at the right quality, with the pipeline you have?
- Team – key people, experience level, turnover, burnout, people split across multiple projects.
- Dependencies – external partners, platforms, certification, IP owners, middleware, funding milestones.
- Schedule – fixed external dates, slips that cascade into marketing or partner problems.

If your risk list only talks about technology, you're missing most of what can actually kill or delay the game.

A simple Top 5 risk format

You don't need a giant risk register.
Start with five biggest risks and capture three things for each:

- Risk – what might realistically go wrong? Say it in one clear sentence.
- Why it matters – what happens if this blows up? Time, money, quality, people, reputation.
- First mitigation step – one concrete, small action you can take now, not a vague "we'll be careful".

You're not trying to solve everything on paper but you trying to move from "we hope it's fine" to "we're doing at least one real thing about it".

Try this

On the right page, write your Top 5 risks for the game you're working on now:
1.For each risk, fill in:

- Risk:
- Why it matters:
- First mitigation step:

2.Check your list against the buckets above.
If all five are technical, ask yourself:
"What could go wrong with players, content, people, partners, or dates?"
3.Look at your mitigation steps and ask:
"Can someone start this this week?"
If not, the step is too vague. Make it smaller and more concrete.

If your pitch deck can't survive an honest "Top Risks" slide, your plan is fragile – not your risk list.

Watch out for

- A risk list with no actions – that's just a fear log, not management.
- Treating risks as something you hide because they might "ruin the pitch". Serious partners trust teams who see the problems early.
- Focusing only on what might break in the engine, and ignoring what might break in the team, the plan or the market.
- Writing this page once and never revisiting it when scope, budget, team or deadlines change.

You don't get to choose whether risks exist, but you can choose whether you and your team talk about them in time to do something.

Topic: .... Date: ....

What Success Looks Like

If you don't define what success means for this game, everything will feel urgent and nothing will feel finished.
If "success" only means money for someone above you, you're missing most of the picture.
A real success definition is multi-dimensional:

- the business outcome,
- what happens to your players,
- what happens to your team,
- what kind of product you're proud to ship.

It also has to fit inside your constraints and support your USP.
If your success story ignores your real box or contradicts what makes the game special, it's just a fantasy.

Four angles of success

You don't need perfect KPIs here but a clear picture of what "this went well" means in practice.

Business – is this game worth it for the company?
Think about sustainable revenue and impact, not just a one-line "make lots of money".
For example: healthy sales for its size and niche, recouping development in a reasonable time, enough success to justify support or a next project in this space.
Players – did this game land for the people it's for?
Is there really something valuable for the player.
For example: players finishing the game at levels you're happy with, decent ratings and reviews, a community that feels more alive than toxic, people recommending the game to friends.
Team – what did this project do to the people making it?
If the game "succeeds" while the team burns out and wants to quit, that's not a real win.
For example: shipping without endless death marches, people willing to stay for the next project, a sense that the team learned and grew instead of just surviving.
Product – does the game stand on its own feet?
This is about quality and craft at the level that makes sense for your scope and niche.
For example: a stable build, coherent design, no catastrophic issues at launch, a game you're not ashamed to show in a portfolio or talk about publicly.

Each of these angles should give you a few short sentences, not a spreadsheet.
Later, you can turn some of them into hard numbers if you need to. Here, focus on clarity first.

Try this
On the right page, define success for your current game:

- For Business, write one or two sentences starting with:

"It's a success for the company if..."

- For Players, write one or two sentences starting with:

"It's a success for our players if..."

- For Team, write one or two sentences starting with:

"It's a success for the team if..."

- For Product, write one or two sentences starting with:

"It's a success for the game itself if..."
Then look at your constraints and USP and ask:

- "Can this picture of success realistically happen inside our real box?"
- "Does this picture of success match what we claim makes this game worth playing?"

If not, adjust the vision, the constraints, or the success picture. Leaving them misaligned guarantees pain later.

Watch out for

- Success definitions that only mention money, with nothing about players, team or quality.
- Goals that are clearly impossible given your time, budget and people – everyone feels the lie.
- Copy-pasting generic targets ("great reviews", "strong community") with no thought about your niche and scale.
- Never revisiting success metrics when the project changes direction, scope or resources.

Good success metrics help you say no to work that doesn't matter and yes to the few things that actually move you toward the outcome you want.

Topic: .... Date: ....

Block B
Planning & Scoping

Topic: .... Date: ....

Roadmap, Milestones & Sprints – Who Does What

"Plan" means very different things depending on how far you look ahead.
If you treat the roadmap like a sprint backlog, you will burn everyone out.
If you treat a sprint like a roadmap, you'll never know if you're actually getting closer to launch.
You need three levels that work together:

- Roadmap – direction.
- Milestones – big steps.
- Sprints – what we're doing right now.

Three levels on one page

Level	Horizon	Questions it answers	Who cares most
Roadmap	Months to whole project	Where are we going? In what order, roughly?	Producers, leads, leadership, partners, team
Milestones	Weeks to a few months	What has to be true by this point?	Producers, leads, partner contacts
Sprints	Days to 1–3 weeks	What do we work on next, concretely?	Whole dev team, producer, discipline leads

- The roadmap shows the big phases and major bets, not individual tasks.
- Milestones turn the roadmap into check points where you review and decide.
- Sprints are the short cycles where work actually happens.

Each level should be readable on its own and consistent with the others.

Typical mix-ups (and why they hurt)

A few patterns to watch for:

- Using the roadmap as a task list – leads to over-detailed promises far in the future that you can't possibly keep.
- Treating sprints as a dumping ground for every idea and request – nothing feels truly planned, everything is "ASAP".
- Having milestones that are just dates, with no clear goal or decision – the team "hits the date" but nobody really checks where the game is.

When people don't know which level a decision belongs to, planning turns into noise.

Try this

Use the right page for your current game:

- Write one or two lines that describe your roadmap in plain language.
- Write one or two lines that describe the next milestone and what must be true at that point.
- Write one or two lines that describe what a sprint means for your team (length, purpose, outcome).

Then pick one real decision you're facing now (for example, adding a new feature, moving a date, changing scope) and note:
At which level does this decision belong – roadmap, milestone, or sprint?

If the answer is "all of them", break it down until each level has a clear, different role in that decision.

Watch out for

- Using the roadmap as a glorified task list – stuffing it with detailed tickets months in advance and then being punished for every change.
- Sprints with no clear goal – just "more work" every week, no theme, no learning, no visible progress to show.
- Milestones that are only dates – "we hit the date" but nobody checks what the game can actually do now.
- Decisions made at the wrong level – changing roadmap direction in a sprint planning, or burying milestone decisions deep inside task discussions.

If people around you say "the plan" and mean different things, stop and clarify which level you're talking about before you argue about it.

Topic: .... Date: ....

High-Level Roadmap Draft

A roadmap is not a promise to hit exact dates.
It's a shared, high-level guess about direction, order and focus for the next months of the project.
On one page you want to see: what big phases you expect, what each phase is roughly for, and how that fits your scope, your constraints and your definition of success. If that picture doesn't fit your real box, the roadmap is lying to you.

Phases – pick what fits your game

You don't have to use the same phases every time.
Pick 3–5 phases that match the scope and shape of your project and name them in a way your team recognises.

For many games, it looks roughly like this:
- Prototype – prove the core idea and loop are worth building.
- Pre-Production – lock key decisions: vision, core systems, style, tools, basic content plan.
- Production – build and integrate content and systems at scale.
- Beta / Polish – stabilise, fix, tune, clean up, prepare for launch and certification.
- Launch / Early Live – ship, watch what happens, fix critical issues, learn.

If your game is tiny, you may collapse phases.

If your game is big or live-heavy, you may split some phases further. The labels matter less than being honest about what each phase is for.

What must be clear on a roadmap

For each phase on the roadmap, you want a short, readable summary:
- Main goal – what this phase is supposed to achieve (in plain language).
- Key focus areas – 2–3 themes, not task lists.
- Major risks to watch – what you're still unsure about going into this phase.
- Rough timing – an approximate window, not fake precision dates.

The roadmap should be high-level enough that it doesn't collapse the moment reality moves, and concrete enough that people can see what comes before what.
Fake precise dates that ignore your constraints will impress no one in the long run.
If you put them in just to look serious, you're only setting yourself up to lose trust later.

Try this

On the right page, sketch a one-page roadmap for your current game:
- Draw a simple horizontal line and mark 3–5 phases that make sense for your project and scope.
- For each phase, write one sentence:
- "In this phase, we mainly focus on..."
- Under the line, write one short note on how this roadmap fits:
  - your constraints (time, budget, team, tech),
  - your success picture (what you want out of this game).

Then ask yourself:
- "Looking at this roadmap, what do we clearly not have time or capacity for?"
- "If we insist on keeping everything, which part of reality are we ignoring?"

If the roadmap doesn't force any trade-offs, it's not a real roadmap yet.

Watch out for
- Turning the roadmap into a detailed task schedule months in advance.
- Adding exact dates you know are made up, just to make the slide look good.
- Planning phases that completely ignore your constraints or your USP – you can't roadmap your way out of a box you refuse to see.
- Never updating the roadmap when scope, budget or team change; an outdated roadmap quietly damages trust.

Topic: .... Date: ....

What a Good Milestone Looks Like

A milestone is not just a date someone circled in a calendar.
A milestone without a real decision attached is just a date someone will be angry about.
Whether it's internal or agreed with a partner, a good milestone is a moment to inspect the game and decide what to do next. Sometimes that decision is about budget and scope, sometimes about quality and direction, sometimes about whether you keep going at all – but there should always be a concrete, iterative decision on the table.

What a milestone really is

A milestone should help you answer questions like:

- "What can the game actually do now?"
- "What did we learn since the previous milestone?"
- "Given what we see, what do we change, cut or double down on for the next phase?"

The shape of a milestone can differ – prototype review, vertical slice, content-complete, beta-ready – but the core idea stays the same: you look at evidence, talk honestly about it, and adjust the plan.

Core elements of a good milestone

A useful milestone usually has:

- A clear goal – one or two sentences in plain language: what this milestone is supposed to prove or unlock.
- Concrete deliverables – what will exist in the game or around it (build, tools, documents, content) at this point.
- Material you can review – something you can actually play, watch, test or evaluate, not only a list of "done" tasks.
- Specific questions and risks to check – what you want to learn or de-risk by this point.
- An explicit decision afterwards – go / adjust / cut / stop; what changes in the plan based on what you just saw.

Different studios and partners may use the word "milestone" in slightly different ways, but if there is no evidence and no decision, it's not a real milestone – it's just a checkpoint on a Gantt chart.

A simple milestone template

On the right page, you can describe any milestone using this simple structure:

- Name – a short label everyone uses in conversations.
- Goal – what this milestone is for; what you want to prove, see, or unlock.
- Deliverables – what will be ready to show or use (build, features, content, tools, docs).
- Risks to check – a few bullets on which uncertainties you expect to reduce here.
- Decision after – what you want to decide at this point (continue as planned, change scope, move dates, cut features, stop).

You can add extra fields if your situation needs them (for example Audience – internal / partner / platform), but these basics should stay short and readable on one page.

Try this

Take your next upcoming milestone and rewrite it using the template:

- Write the Name and Goal in plain language.
- List only the Deliverables that someone will actually review.
- Note Risks to check – what this milestone should make less scary or unknown.
- Write one line for Decision after:
- "After this milestone, we will decide whether to..."

Then ask yourself:

- "If we hit all deliverables but don't make a clear decision, would this milestone still be useful?"
- If the honest answer is "no", adjust the definition until the decision is obvious.

Watch out for

- Milestones that are only dates – "we reached 31st of March" is not a result.
- Milestones defined purely as task lists – everything "Done" in the tracker, but nobody really looks at the game or the risks.
- Milestones that are endlessly pushed back without changing scope or expectations – the label moves, the underlying problem stays the same.

A good milestone lets you look at the game, learn something real, and change the plan on purpose – not by accident.

Topic: .... Date: ....

Breaking Features Down

Big features sound impressive in meetings. They're much less impressive when nobody knows what exactly needs to be done next.
A card called "New Co-op Mode" or "Improve Progression" on your board is not a plan. If your "feature" can't be broken into clear tasks, you don't really understand it yet – and your team definitely doesn't.
Breaking work down is not bureaucracy. It's how you turn vision, pillars and constraints into something people can actually ship.

From Epic to Features to Tasks

Think in three simple levels:

- Epic – a larger theme or capability ("Photo Mode").
- Features – distinct pieces of functionality inside that epic ("Taking a shot", "Viewing shots", "Basic sharing").
- Tasks – concrete steps someone can do and mark as done.

A quick, simple example:

- Epic: Photo Mode
    - Feature: Capture flow
        - Tasks: define the flow (enter/exit), implement capture, simple feedback when a shot is taken.
    - Feature: Gallery
        - Tasks: show list of shots, open single shot, delete shot.
    - Feature: Camera controls & UI
        - Tasks: basic camera movement, a minimal HUD, mapping input to actions.

The names don't need to be perfect. What matters is that each level tells people something useful about scope and next steps.
Keep the breakdown aligned with your game pillars, USP and constraints. There's no point in exploding an epic into 50 tasks if half of them don't support what makes your game worth playing or don't fit your real box.

What makes a good task
A useful task is:

- Clear – one person can read it and know what "done" looks like.
- Testable – you can check if it works in the game or in a tool.
- Small enough – it fits into a reasonable chunk of time, not "two months".
- Owned – someone is clearly responsible, even if more people help.

Bad task examples you want to avoid:

- "Make UI"
- "Polish level"
- "Balance weapons"
- "Fix stuff in tutorial"

These hide real work instead of exposing it. They create arguments later about whether something is "actually done".

Try this
On the right page, take one real "big thing" from your current project and break it down:

- Write it as an Epic (one short line).
- Under it, list 2–3 Features – each a distinct part of that epic that a player could notice.
- For each feature, write 3–5 tasks that are small, clear and testable.

Then look at your list and ask:

- "Would a new team member understand what these tasks mean?"
- "Do these tasks move us toward our pillars and USP, or are we just adding noise?"

If the answer is "I'm not sure", sharpen the wording until it's obvious.

Watch out for

- Epics that stay on the board for months with no real breakdown – permanent "ghost work" nobody owns.
- Task names that are just labels for anxiety ("Optimize everything", "Fix all bugs").
- Breaking things down in a way that ignores constraints – dozens of tasks you realistically have no time or people for.
- Spending hours wordsmithing tasks instead of getting them just clear enough and moving on.

Breaking features down is not about being perfect on paper. It's about making the next steps real and visible so the game can actually move forward.

Topic: .... Date: ....

Prioritisation Basics (MoSCoW / RICE)

If everything is "high priority", nothing is.
Prioritisation is mainly about deciding what you won't do now – or won't do at all.
The goal is not a perfect formula. The goal is a clear, honest way to say:

- what must happen first,
- what can wait,
- what should be dropped because it doesn't fit your pillars, USP or constraints.

If an item doesn't support what makes your game worth playing, or doesn't fit your real box of time / people / budget, it has no right to sit in Must.

MoSCoW – simple buckets for "now vs later"
MoSCoW splits work into four buckets:

- Must – without this, the game or milestone fails its purpose.
- Should – important and valuable, but survivable if delayed.
- Could – nice-to-have if there is free space; first to cut when reality hits.
- Won't (for now) – explicit "not now / maybe never"; parked on purpose, not forgotten by accident.

The power of MoSCoW is not the labels. It's the fact that "Won't for now" is allowed and visible, instead of pretending everything fits.

RICE – a quick sanity check
RICE gives you four lenses to compare items, without pretending to be perfect math:

- Reach – how many players / sessions / situations does this affect?
- Impact – how strongly does it change those players' experience?
- Confidence – how sure are you about your assumptions (high / medium / low)?
- Effort – how heavy is this compared to other work (small / medium / large)?

You don't have to calculate scores.

You can simply ask for each item:

- Is Reach / Impact / Confidence / Effort -------------- high / medium / low?

Then compare: something with high reach + high impact + small/medium effort is a much better candidate for Must than something niche, unclear and expensive.

How to actually decide
A few simple rules help:

- Someone has to own the decision – usually a producer / lead – or you'll argue forever.
- That person should be hard on criteria, soft with people: listening to good feedback, but not letting the loudest voice win.
- Bring in pillars, USP and constraints explicitly:

"Does this feature support our pillars?", "Does it help show our USP?", "Does it fit our time, team and budget?"

- Write decisions down. If everything lives only in conversation, priorities will drift back to chaos.

Prioritisation is not about being nice to every idea. It's about being fair to the game and to the team.

Try this
On the right page, take a real list of features or tasks from your current project and:

- Mark each item as Must / Should / Could / Won't for now.
- For 3–5 biggest items, quickly note RICE in words, e.g.:

Reach, Impact, Confidence, Effort -------------- high / medium / low

- Check your Must column and ask:

"Does each Must clearly support our pillars and USP?", "Can we realistically do all these Musts inside our constraints?"
If the answer is "no", you don't have priorities – you have a wish list.

Watch out for

- Treating everything as Must because nobody wants to say no.
- Skipping "Won't for now" – parked work comes back anyway, but now as hidden scope creep.
- Letting the most stressed or loud person decide what's important.
- Ignoring pillars, USP and constraints – if you prioritise without them, you're optimising the wrong game.

Good prioritisation is not about being perfect. It's about giving your team permission to focus on the few things that actually matter now.

Topic: ....   Date: ....

Definition of Done That Prevents Surprises

If "Done" means something different in everyone's head, nothing is really done.
"Done" is not "it compiles on my machine".
A clear Definition of Done protects you from hidden work, unpleasant surprises, and fake progress.
You don't need a giant checklist. You need a short, shared agreement of what "finished enough to move on" means – for a feature and for a milestone.

Definition of Done for a feature

For a feature, "Done" should mean that a player (or tester) can actually use it in the game, not just that some code exists.
A feature is usually Done when:

- It is implemented and integrated in the main game build (not in a local branch only).
- It is reachable in normal play or through a simple test path (no secret console magic only one dev knows).
- It behaves according to the current design/acceptance criteria – good enough for this phase.
- It has passed basic testing (at least smoke tests and obvious edge cases).
- It doesn't introduce new blockers or obvious crashes for other parts of the game.

If there's always "a bit more wiring, a bit more UI, a bit more tuning" after "Done", your Definition of Done is too weak.

Definition of Done for a milestone

For a milestone, "Done" is not "most tasks are closed".
A milestone is Done when you can look at the game and honestly answer:
"Did we achieve the goal we set for this milestone?"
A milestone is usually Done when:

- The agreed goal for this milestone has been reached in the real build.
- The key deliverables exist in a form that can be played, watched or reviewed (not only described).
- The planned checks/risks for this milestone have actually been inspected (not skipped "to save time").
- There is a short review + decision: what we change, cut or double down on for the next phase.

If a milestone "passes" without anyone really looking at the game, you don't have a milestone – you have a moving calendar entry.

Hidden work after "Done"

A weak Definition of Done creates invisible tails of work:

- "Done" feature that still needs connecting to inputs, tutorial, UI, save/load, analytics.
- "Done" milestone that still needs builds prepared, store pages updated, trailers captured, materials sent to partners.

Your Definition of Done should pull this work into the light.
If something always has to happen after "Done" before people can truly use or ship it, add a simple line so it's part of Done, not a surprise.

Try this

On the right page, write your own Definition of Done:

1. For features – list 5–7 short conditions that must be true before you call a feature Done in your project.
2. For milestones – list 5–7 short conditions that must be true before you say a milestone is Done.
3. Look at your last "finished" feature / milestone and check:
   - Which of these conditions were actually met?
   - Which ones were quietly skipped?

Adjust your Definition of Done until it matches how you want to work, not just how you accidentally worked last time.

Watch out for

- "Done" meaning only "the code is written" – integration, testing and usability still missing.
- Big chunks of standard work left outside the definition: documentation, builds, platform prep, basic UX polish.
- Everyone using the word "Done" but meaning something different – designers, programmers, QA, producer.
- Making the checklist so long that nobody ever reads it – keep it short, clear, and actually used in everyday discussions.

Topic: .... Date: ....

Spotting Scope Creep Early

Scope creep is not a surprise. It's a series of small "yes" decisions nobody wanted to own.
It rarely shows up as "we added a huge new feature". It shows up as:
"just one more option", "just a small extra system", "just a few more levels", "we'll make it nicer later".
Each one alone looks harmless. Together they quietly destroy your roadmap, milestones and priorities.
Scope creep itself isn't evil. Unmanaged scope creep is. Small changes are fine if they go through your roadmap, milestones and prioritisation – and if something else drops out to make space.

Typical symptoms of scope creep

You might already be in scope creep territory if:

- More work keeps entering the project than leaving it – your lists grow even when people are "busy all the time".
- There is no time for polish – you're always building new things, rarely finishing existing ones.
- "Quick changes" keep bypassing the roadmap, milestones and Must/Should/Could buckets.
- Milestones are pushed forward with the same scope instead of being adjusted.
- The game in your head (or decks) is drifting away from what's actually realistic for your team and constraints.

If you feel you're always saying "yes, but later" and "later" never comes, it's a red flag.

Simple reaction loop: notice → name → re-balance

When you see scope creep, don't just complain. Run a quick loop:

- Notice

Say out loud that something is being added:
"We're talking about adding a new X on top of what we already planned."

- Name

Attach it somewhere visible: roadmap, milestone, or the same feature list you prioritise from.
If it's not worth writing down, it's probably not worth doing.
Re-balance using priorities and ask a few blunt questions:

  - Does this support our pillars and USP?
  - Is this more important than something already in Must?
  - What do we drop, delay or simplify to make space?

Small changes are okay if they follow this logic:
something new comes in → something else moves out or down.
If nothing ever moves out or down, you're not re-balancing – you're just inflating the scope.

Try this
On the right page, look at your current project and:

1. Write down 3 recent examples where something was added "on top": a feature, a level, a system, a "quick tweak".
2. For each, note:
   - Where it should live (roadmap / milestone / sprint list).
   - Whether something else was explicitly cut or delayed when you added it.
3. Circle the cases where scope grew without any trade-off. That's your live scope creep.

Then pick one of them and decide now:

- Do we keep it and cut/delay something else?
- Or do we park it in "Won't for now" and stop pretending we're doing everything?

Watch out for

- Saying "yes" to everything because it's "small" – hundreds of small things sink more projects than a few big ones.
- Letting scope creep happen in conversations only, with no update to roadmap, milestones or priority lists.
- Using buffer as a silent safety net for all extra ideas, instead of protecting it for real unknowns.
- Treating any attempt to cut or delay work as a personal attack, instead of a normal part of production.

Scope will always try to grow. Your job is not to stop every new idea – it's to make sure every "yes" comes with a conscious trade-off.

Topic: .... Date: ....

Vertical Slice Without the Myth

A vertical slice is not "half the game".
It's a small, playable piece that proves the real game is worth finishing.
For many teams (and partners) a vertical slice is a milestone with a special job:
show that the core loop, the key systems and the quality bar actually work together on real content – not just in slides and prototypes.
If your vertical slice can't be built without wrecking the rest of the plan, it's badly defined.

What a vertical slice really is
A good VS answers a few simple questions:

- "Is our core loop actually fun/interesting enough to build a whole game around?"
- "Can our key systems work together at something close to target quality?"
- "Does the look, feel and UX of this game make sense when everything is on screen at once?"

It's not about size. It's about representativeness: a thin cut through the real game, not a tech demo or a random prototype.
In many projects, the VS is tied to an important milestone – internal or with a partner – where you review the slice and decide: continue, adjust, or rethink.

What must be in a vertical slice
You don't need every system. You do need a believable, end-to-end experience for one small segment of the game.
Usually that means:

- A playable core loop – the player can go through the main "do → get feedback → decide what next" cycle at least a few times.
- A few key systems at close-to-target quality – whatever defines your game (e.g. movement/combat, cooking/crafting, building/management...) working together, not in isolation.
- A small, representative piece of content – one mission, one level, one short session, one scenario that feels like the game you want to ship.
- A sample of final look & feel – art, audio and UX good enough that you can honestly say "this is roughly what launch will feel like" on this small slice.

If someone can play your VS and say "I understand what this game is trying to be and how it will feel when finished", you're close.

What does not need to be in a vertical slice
A vertical slice is not your full content plan squeezed into a single date.
You usually do not need:

- Full amount of content – not all levels, all weapons, all biomes, all missions. A few strong examples are enough.
- Every possible UI screen or flow – focus on the ones the slice actually needs.
- Full progression and meta – you can fake some parts as long as the core experience is honest.
- Full optimisation and porting to every platform – stability matters, micro-optimisation later.

If you try to cram "almost everything" into VS, you're building half a game with half the time. That's how teams burn months on one milestone and still don't really know if the game works.

Try this
On the right page, sketch the vertical slice for your current game in 3–4 points:

- Describe the player flow in one short paragraph: what they do from start to finish in the slice.
- List the core systems that must be present and talking to each other in this slice.
- Note what quality bar you're aiming for here (visuals, audio, UX) – "good enough for VS" in plain language.
- Write one sentence:
- "After this vertical slice milestone, we want to decide whether to..."

Then ask yourself:

- "Can we build this slice inside our real time and team?"
- "If not, what can we shrink without losing the truth of the game?"
-

Watch out for

- Treating VS as "trade show demo only" – beautiful but disconnected from the real game structure.
- Designing the whole production around impressing one VS milestone, instead of serving the full game afterwards.
- Making the slice so small and rough that it doesn't prove anything about real gameplay or quality.
- Forgetting that VS is still a milestone: it needs a clear goal, review and decision, not just "we survived another date".

A good vertical slice is a honest preview of the game you are actually able to ship – on a small, sharp, playable piece.

Topic: .... Date: ....

Simple Content Plan

Most projects underestimate content.
"We'll add more later" usually means "we'll crunch later" or "we'll ship something thinner than we promised."
You don't need a complex spreadsheet here. You need a clear, realistic picture of how much content your game needs to feel complete for your target player – and how much work that implies for your team.
In an iterative medium like gamedev, some content will be changed, thrown away or reworked. A good content plan assumes that from the start, instead of pretending every first attempt will ship.

Think in content types, not asset names

Keep it neutral so it works across genres. Typical buckets:

- Spaces / locations – levels, areas, rooms, arenas, hubs, maps, any place where play happens.
- Interactive things – enemies, NPCs, items, props, machines, puzzles, systems you can touch or use.
- Authored experiences – quests, missions, events, scenarios, waves, story beats, challenges.

For each type, you want to roughly answer:

- How many of these does the player need to feel they got a full experience?
- How many can your team realistically build and polish within your constraints?

Your goal is not perfect numbers. Your goal is to stop saying "we'll see" and start saying "we're aiming at this scale, and that has consequences".

Count, then respect the iteration

For each content type:

- Start from experience – yours or someone you trust:
- "Games of this scope usually need about X locations / encounters / missions to feel complete."
- Translate that into a target range, not a single magic number.
- Accept that some percentage will be reworked or thrown away as you test and learn.

Gamedev is an iterative process. Some content will be cut because it's boring, redundant, or simply weaker than the rest. That's normal. A realistic plan:

- counts that content will be created and then dropped,
- leaves space for a few extra pieces to replace the weak ones,
- doesn't rely on "every first attempt ships".

If every single piece of content you make ends up in the final game, you probably didn't experiment or cut enough.

Try this

On the right page, sketch a simple content plan for your current game:

1. List 3–4 content types that matter most (e.g. "core spaces", "key interactive elements", "authored experiences").
2. For each type, write:
   - "Target range we're aiming for" – a realistic band, not a fantasy number.
   - One note on why this range makes sense (based on similar games, your past experience, or someone you trust).
3. Add one line at the bottom:

"We expect some portion of this content to be reworked or cut as we iterate – and that's built into this plan."
Then look at your roadmap and team and ask:

- "If we're honest about iteration, do we still have enough time and people to reach this scale?"
- "If not, what do we need to shrink now, before we lie to ourselves and the team?"

Watch out for

- Saying "we'll just add more later" with no idea how many or who will build it.
- Planning content as if nothing will ever be cut or redone.
- A plan that ignores your team size, experience and tools – counting content as if you had a completely different studio.
- Hiding content decisions inside features ("new mode", "new system") instead of asking:
- "How many actual playable pieces does this mean for us?"

A simple, honest content plan won't make production easy, but it will at least make the difficulty visible while you can still do something about it.

Topic: .... Date: ....

Balancing Tech Debt and New Features

If you never plan time for tech debt, you're planning future crises.
Only adding new features on top of a shaky base is not progress – it's a slow disaster you're scheduling for later.
Tech debt is not just "ugly code". It's anything in your game or tools that makes future changes more expensive and painful than they need to be: brittle systems, unstable builds, bad performance, fragile pipelines. A good producer / tech lead doesn't pretend debt doesn't exist; they decide when and how to pay it down without turning the whole project into a refactor party.

What tech debt really is (in production terms)
Think in a few simple buckets:

- Stability & bugs – crashes, blockers, edge cases everyone knows about but nobody has time to fix.
- Performance – framerate, loading, memory, hitches that will only get worse as you add content.
- Tools & pipeline – slow import times, broken exporters, manual processes that eat hours every week.
- Fragile architecture – systems that are so tangled that any change risks breaking three other things.

Some level of tech debt is normal and even strategic: you cut corners now to learn fast, knowing you'll revisit later. The danger comes when those "later" passes never happen and debt silently dictates what you can and cannot ship.

Conscious tech passes instead of permanent emergency
You don't have to treat tech debt as background guilt. You can plan explicit tech passes – focused cycles where the main goal is to stabilise, clean up and buy back flexibility.
A good tech pass:

- Has a clear goal, like "stabilise builds and crash rate" or "make level iteration 2× faster", not "fix all tech debt".
- Is time-boxed – one sprint, one milestone, a defined window, not "we'll refactor until it feels good".
- Targets a few high-impact debts that unlock smoother feature work afterwards.
- Ends with a visible before/after: fewer crashes, faster iteration, fewer manual steps.

You don't stop making features forever; you accept that sometimes the healthiest thing you can do for the game and the team is to slow feature growth down and fix the foundation you're standing on.
Each team will need a different balance. Your job is to decide that balance on purpose, write it down, and revisit it when reality changes – not to improvise it from crisis to crisis.

Tech debt and new features on the same board
Tech debt shouldn't live in a separate, invisible list. Put significant debts on the same board or tracker as features, and talk about them with the same seriousness:

- When you plan a milestone or sprint, look at both: planned features and the worst debts.
- Ask, as producers and tech leads together:
  - "If we ignore this debt, what will happen in 2–3 months?"
  - "Does this piece of debt block or slow down multiple features?"
- Decide where a tech pass fits into the roadmap, and what you're willing to delay to make it happen.

Healthy production doesn't pretend you can have maximum new features and zero time for debt. It recognises that a small sacrifice now often prevents a much bigger sacrifice later.

Try this
On the right page, make a simple snapshot for your current project:

- List three biggest tech debts that hurt you today (stability, performance, tools or architecture).
- List three new features you're planning for the next milestone or two.
- For each tech debt, write one short line: "If we ignore this, it will cost us later by..."
- Decide on one conscious tech pass in the near future: when it should happen, which debts it will focus on, which features or tasks will move out to make space.

If you can't move anything out, you're not really planning a tech pass – you're adding more expectations on top of the same capacity.

Watch out
A team that always "does debt later" drifts into a pattern where every change is risky, every build feels unstable, and every new feature takes longer than it should. On papier everything looks fine – roadmap, milestones, feature lists – but underneath, people are scared to touch whole parts of the code or content because they know it might explode. On the other side, a team that hides behind tech debt to avoid decisions will spend months polishing internals that never translate into better builds, clearer workflows or a stronger game. The balance you want is simple: you acknowledge debt early, you speak about it in the same room as features, you sometimes stop to run a focused tech pass, and you are honest about what has to wait so that the foundation can survive the rest of the project.

Topic: .... Date: ....

Budget Awareness for Non-Finance People

If you ignore budget, you're still making budget decisions – just blindly.
You don't need to love spreadsheets. But as a producer or lead, you do need a basic feel for what things cost in time and money.
Budget, at this level, is simply: how long which people work on this game, plus a few obvious external costs. That's it. You don't need formulas to start thinking clearly.

What a budget really means in production

For most teams, the budget is made from a few simple pieces:

- People time – how many people are on the project, and for how many months.
- External work – outsourcing, freelancers, QA services, ports.
- Tools and services – engine licenses, plugins, servers, middleware, external builds/tests.
- Launch and beyond – marketing support, trailers, PR assets, platform requirements.

You don't have to know exact numbers, but you should have a rough sense of scale:
"Keeping this team on this project for one more month" is not free. It's one more month of salary, one more month you're not shipping or starting the next thing.
On bigger projects you will need better tools and help from finance. But the starting point is always the same: people × time, plus some extra lines for external stuff.

How production decisions hit the budget

Every time you say things like "let's add one more person", "let's do another sprint", "let's outsource this part", you are changing the budget. Saying "it's just a small change" doesn't make it cheap.
When you extend a milestone, you're effectively buying more time from the team. When you add a feature late, you're paying not only for building it, but also for testing, fixing, and maintaining it. When you accept a partner request, you're committing real people for real days.

You don't need to quote numbers in every conversation, only try to build a habit of silently asking yourself:

- "How many person-days or person-weeks is this likely to cost?"
- "If we spend that here, what won't we spend it on?"

That alone will make your planning more honest.

Try this

On the right page, do a quick "napkin budget" for your current situation:

1. Write how many people are effectively on this game right now, and for roughly how long you expect them to stay. Add a short line: "One extra month with this team = X person-months more."
2. Pick one real decision on the table (extra sprint, new feature, small outsourcing package) and describe, in words, how it affects the budget: more time, more people, or extra external cost.
3. Underneath, answer two questions:
    - "If we do this, what do we have to delay, shrink or drop to keep the budget sane?"
    - "If we don't do this, what risk or opportunity are we accepting?"

You don't need exact amounts, but you need to stop pretending there is no trade-off.

Watch out

When nobody talks about budget, scope grows "for free" – until suddenly it doesn't, and you're forced into last-minute cuts and crunch. When only one person in the studio understands the numbers, everyone else treats cost as magic and throws ideas over the wall. What you want instead is simple: producers and leads who can think in terms of people and time, who know that every extra sprint, feature or headcount line has a price, and who are willing to say "this is not small, let's decide what we are sacrificing to pay for it."

Topic: .... Date: ....

Buffers That Are Actually Used

If you plan at 100% capacity with no buffers, you're not planning – you're hoping for a miracle.
Buffers and contingency are not laziness. They're an honest admission that game development is messy: people get sick, tools break, features are harder than expected, platforms change requirements. A good plan assumes this and still leaves room to breathe.
You can buffer in three simple ways: time, scope, and people. You don't need complicated math. You need a plan that doesn't fall apart at the first surprise.

Time buffers – breathing room before hard dates

Time buffers sit before hard external dates, not after them.
If you have a platform submission, a marketing beat or a launch window, your internal "ready" date should be earlier than that external date. The gap between them is your contingency for last-minute fixes, build issues and missing assets.
Practical rule of thumb: plan your work so that the team is not booked to 100%. A roadmap or milestone plan where every week is full and nothing can slip is a fantasy. Real plans have a bit of slack, especially close to big decision points and external deadlines.

Scope buffers – things you're ready to cut

Scope buffers are features, content or polish that you would like to have, but are explicitly marked as the first to cut if reality hits.
They are not secret dreams hidden in the backlog. They are visible, agreed "if we have time" items. When things slip, you don't pretend you can still do everything – you immediately look at scope buffers and start removing or delaying them.
A strong scope buffer is connected to your prioritisation: Must / Should / Could. The Could items are not "maybe magically for free later"; they are your contingency. When something unexpected appears, you cut here first instead of pushing every date forward.

People buffers – not running everyone at 100%

People are not CPUs you can safely run at 100% load all the time.
When you plan every person's capacity to the last hour, you leave no room for support work, mentoring, context switches, bugs, meetings, or just a bad day. Over a few weeks this turns into hidden overtime or slow, silent burnout.
Healthy planning assumes that across a milestone or sprint, people will have less than 100% of their time available for "planned work" and that some of their energy will go into unplanned issues. You don't have to put a number on it; you just need to stop pretending that fully packed boards are realistic.

Try this

On the right page, sketch buffers for your current project:

- Mark one or two time buffers: where in your roadmap or milestone plan you will stop adding new work so there is room for fixes before an external date.
- List a small scope buffer: a handful of features or content you would be willing to cut or delay first, if you start slipping.
- Note your people reality in one or two sentences: how much unplanned work tends to appear in a typical week, and what that means for how "full" you can safely plan.

Then look at your current plan and ask:

- "If one key thing takes longer than expected, do we have anywhere for that time to come from?"
- "If not, where will we steal it from – and why not be honest about that now?"

Watch out

A buffer that is immediately filled on day one is not a buffer, it's self-deception. A plan that books everyone to the limit and assumes every feature lands exactly on time is already broken, just not yet visible. And a team that treats any mention of contingency as weakness will end up paying for it later in crunch, slipped milestones or rushed cuts. The point of buffers is simple: you admit that unpredictable things will happen and you decide in advance where the extra time, scope and energy will come from, instead of improvising under pressure.

Topic: .... Date: ....

Production Modes and How They Change the Work

If you act like you're in pre-production while claiming you're in production, you're lying to yourself and your team.
Each phase of a project has a different purpose and a different kind of work. When those don't match, plans and expectations fall apart.
You don't need perfect definitions. You do need a shared language for what it means to be in Pre-production, Production, Beta or Live, so you can plan scope and pace accordingly.

Pre-production – prove the game is worth building
Pre-production is where you discover the game. The main job is to reduce uncertainty: find the core loop, check your pillars, understand roughly who you're building for and whether the idea holds up when it's playable, not just on slides.
Work in this mode is experiment-heavy: prototypes, ugly builds, fast changes, throwing things away on purpose. Planning is about questions: "What do we need to learn next?" and "What must be true before we go into full production?"
If you refuse to cut bad ideas here, you're pushing expensive problems into the future.

Production – build what you already believe in
Production is where you execute on decisions made in pre-prod. You're scaling up content, systems and tools, not reinventing the core loop every week.
Work in this mode is about throughput and integration: getting features and content from "planned" to "in the build" in a steady rhythm. Planning is more detailed: milestones, content plans, build cadence, definition of done. You still iterate, but within guardrails set by your vision, pillars, constraints and earlier learning.
If you keep behaving like pre-prod in production – constant big changes, no stable targets – you will drown in rework.

Beta – stabilise, tune, prepare to ship
Beta is where you finish the version you're actually going to launch. The main job is to harden the build, fix what hurts players most, smooth the rough edges and make sure the whole thing holds together.
Work in this mode is less about adding big new things and more about: bug fixing, performance, tuning, UX clarity, platform and store requirements, test passes. Planning should narrow: you cut more than you add, and you protect time for polish and stability.
If your beta roadmap is full of brand new features, you're not in beta – you're still in production with a launch date on top.

Live – run and evolve what you shipped
Live is where you operate and evolve the game that is already in players' hands. What "live" means will differ between a premium single-player title and a full live-service game, but in both cases you're dealing with a running product and real audiences.
Work in this mode is driven by data, player behaviour, support and planned updates: patches, events, DLC, content drops, balance passes, tech upkeep. Planning should include an intentional rhythm for updates, tech maintenance, and realistic capacity for new content.
A game that is technically "live" but has no plan for updates, maintenance or player-facing communication is just a project you abandoned after launch. Even a minimal live plan is better than silence and chaos.

Try this
On the right page, write down which mode your current project is truly in: pre-prod, production, beta or live. For that mode, note in a few sentences:

- what the main purpose of the phase is for your game,
- what kind of work should be front and centre right now,
- what kind of work you should say no to or park for later.

Then ask yourself honestly: "Are we behaving like this phase, or like a different one?" If the behaviour and the label don't match, fix the behaviour or change the label – but don't pretend they align when everyone can feel they don't.

Watch out
Staying in pre-production forever – constantly changing the core loop, style or pillars and calling it "exploration" long after you should be making harder choices. At some point you're not discovering anymore, you're avoiding commitment.
Calling it production while behaving like pre-prod – big redesigns every few weeks, shifting targets, no stable content plan. The label doesn't matter if the work is still pure experimentation.
Living in "almost beta" – telling everyone the game is nearly done, but your backlog is full of major new systems and untested content. Beta without a strong focus on stabilising and finishing is just production with extra guilt.
Being live without a plan – the game is out, but there is no clear idea what you'll update, how often, how you'll handle bugs, or how you'll talk to players. A live game with no plan slowly loses trust: inside the team and in the audience. Even a small, realistic live plan is better than pretending launch is the end.

Topic: .... Date: ....

Before You Go Full Production

Going into full production without some basics in place is not being bold – it's betting the whole project on luck.
Pre-production is where you learn what game you're actually making. Production is where you pay for those decisions at scale. This page is here to help you check whether you've learned enough to start paying.
You don't need perfection. You do need enough clarity that going into production is a conscious risk, not self-deception.

What should be true before full production

Use this as a checklist, not a law. But if most of it would be red for you, think very hard before you push the big "Production" button.

1. Clear core loop
You can describe the core loop in one or two sentences that a non-developer understands, and you have at least one build where that loop is playable, not just imagined. When people play it, you get real, repeatable reactions – good or bad. You aren't still arguing about what the player is "mainly doing" in your game.

2. Agreed vision and pillars
The team can roughly agree on what this game wants to be and how it should feel. Your pillars are written down in simple language and actually used when judging ideas. You're not trying to be five different games at once.

3. Basic gameplay holds together
You have a small slice where movement, camera, interaction and feedback work together well enough that you can imagine them scaling. People can pick up a controller / keyboard and play without you explaining every step.

4. Target audience is more than a guess
You know roughly who you're building for and why they would pick this over something else. You've at least tested the idea (and ideally a build) with people close to that audience, not just with your own team.

5. A rough content and feature scale
You have a simple idea of "how much game" you're trying to build: number of spaces, core systems, authored experiences. It doesn't have to be precise, but it has to be honest enough that you can see the difference between "small game" and "huge game".

6. Tech and pipeline can survive scaling
Your engine setup, project structure and tools are good enough that adding more content and systems won't instantly collapse everything. There will still be tech debt and rough edges, but you are not ignoring known fires and pretending they will go away on their own.

Try this
On the right page, write the six headings above (Core loop, Vision & pillars, Basic gameplay, Target audience, Scale, Tech & pipeline).

For each, mark quickly:

- what already feels strong enough for production,
- what is still uncertain or weak,
- what you would need to do in the next weeks to move that area from "dangerous" to "acceptable risk".

Then ask yourself, as honestly as you can:
"If we go into full production now, which of these gaps is most likely to blow up in our face later?"
If the biggest gaps are in core loop, pillars or tech/pipeline, slow down and fix them first. Those cracks only get more expensive when you build the house on top.

Watch out
Teams often rush into production because "we have to show progress" or "everyone is waiting to start building content". It's tempting to pretend that unclear core decisions or painful tech problems will somehow solve themselves once more people are working on the game. They won't. Issues with the loop, pillars or pipeline don't fade in production – they grow teeth. The point of this checklist is not to scare you into waiting forever; it's to stop you from driving a truck full of content and new features onto a road you already know is full of holes.

Topic: .... Date: ....

Handling Change Requests

A "small change" that skips any kind of process is still a big problem.
If every change request is accepted by default, you don't have a plan – you have a wish list.
A change request is any ask to change what you already agreed: scope, behaviour, priorities, dates or quality bar. It doesn't matter whether it comes from someone inside the team, a lead, a partner or a publisher – it all lands in the same reality: your time, your people, your plan.

What a change request really is
Treat every change request as a short story about why the plan should move.
At minimum, you want to know:

- Who is asking – role and responsibility, not just a name.
- What should change – as concrete as possible ("remove X", "replace Y with Z", "add this behaviour").
- Why now – what problem does this fix, what opportunity does it use, what risk does it avoid?
- Impact guess – even a rough sense of how it affects time, scope and risk.

Requests from partners or publishers often come with extra weight (money, contracts, deadlines), but the basics are the same. You still need to understand what changes, why, and what it will cost you in reality.

A simple flow for handling changes
You don't need a heavy formal workflow. You need a light but consistent routine that everyone recognises:

1. Capture

Every change request gets written down somewhere visible (board, document, page in this notebook). No decisions live only in chat logs and hallway conversations.

2. Assess

A decision owner (producer, lead, or whoever you agreed) looks at the request with the right people and asks:

   - How does this affect our scope, time, budget, risk?
   - Does it support our pillars and USP, or is it noise?
   - What would we have to drop, delay or shrink to make space for this?

3. Decide

The decision owner says yes, no, or not now – explicitly. "We'll see later" is often just a slow "yes" without admitting the cost. A clear "no" or "not for this version" is better than permanent maybe.

4. Communicate

The outcome and reasoning are shared with the people who asked and with the team that will be affected. Short and clear is enough: what we're doing, what we're not doing, and why.

If a change is accepted, it should land in the same roadmap, milestone or backlog as everything else, with updated priorities. If it's rejected or deferred, that should be visible too.

Try this
On the right page, start a very simple change request log for your current project. For each new or recent change request, note:

- who asked,
- what they wanted to change,
- why they said it mattered,
- what you decided and how it affects your current plan.

Then look back over the last few weeks and ask yourself:

- "Which changes did we effectively accept without ever writing them down or deciding consciously?"
- "Where did we pay for those hidden changes – extra hours, pushed milestones, cut polish?"
-

If you see a pattern of silent "yes" decisions, this is where you start turning them into visible, owned calls instead of background chaos.

Watch out
Change requests are not the enemy. They are a normal part of making games with real people, real partners and real players. The problem starts when they slip in sideways: agreed in a quick chat, half-promised in a meeting, never attached to any plan, never balanced against other work. Over time, this erodes trust in any roadmap or milestone, because everyone can feel that anything can change at any moment "for free". What you want instead is a culture where changes are captured, someone clearly owns the decision, and every "yes" to a new request comes with an honest adjustment somewhere else.

Topic: .... Date: ....

Outsourcing – When It Actually Helps

Outsourcing badly defined work will not save your project. It will just move the pain to someone else and bring it back later, bigger.
The real question is not "who is cheaper" but "does it make sense for this part of the work to be done by people outside the core team, given our time, focus and risk?". Sometimes the honest answer is yes. Sometimes it's "we're just trying to dodge a problem we should solve in-house".

When outsourcing makes sense

Outsourcing tends to work best when the work is:

- Clear and repeatable – a lot of similar pieces built to a known style or spec, where examples speak louder than long documents.
- Specialised – skills you don't have in-house or don't need full-time (certain art styles, audio, porting, specific tech).
- Decoupled in time – something that can move in parallel without blocking the core team every day.

In those situations, outsourcing can free your team to focus on core gameplay, pillars, and decisions only you can really make.

When you probably shouldn't outsource

Outsourcing is usually a bad fit when the work is:

- Core to what makes the game itself – fundamental design decisions, core tech, systems that define your USP and pillars.
- Still changing every week – if you don't know what you want yet, an external team will mostly generate rework.
- Tightly intertwined with everything else – tasks that need constant back-and-forth with half your team just to move forward.

If you're thinking "let's outsource this because we haven't figured it out and we're late", stop. That's not an outsourcing problem, that's a design/production problem.

The minimum clarity before you talk to anyone

Before you involve an external team, you should be able to write down, in simple language:

- What you want: the type of work, the expected style or behaviour, and a few good and bad examples.
- How much you need: a rough range, not a fantasy number ("about this many pieces / screens / passes").
- What "good enough" looks like: target quality level, not perfection.
- How you will accept the work: who reviews it, in what format, on what schedule, with how many iterations.

This doesn't have to be a legal document. It has to be concrete enough that a competent external team can look at it and say "we understand what you want, and we can or cannot deliver that".

Try this

On the right page, take one area of your current project that you're tempted to outsource and walk through it honestly:

1. Describe the type of work in a few lines (what it is, how it would be used in the game, why you're considering outsourcing it).
2. Answer three questions:
   - Is this work repeatable and well understood, or is it still changing every week?
   - Is it core to our pillars / USP, or more supporting infrastructure or content?
   - What risk do we reduce by outsourcing it, and what risk do we add (communication, quality, delays)?
3. If it still looks like a candidate, sketch a tiny draft scope: what, how much, what "good enough" means, and how you would review deliveries.

If you can't describe the work clearly on this page, you're not ready to outsource it – you're just trying to push ambiguity outside the building.

Watch out

Outsourcing is not a magic button that turns messy work into clean progress. It still needs clear scope, real communication and time from your team to review and integrate what comes back. If you treat it as a way to avoid decisions, you will get exactly that back: someone else's guesses, arriving later than you hoped, forcing you to make decisions under more pressure. Use outsourcing where it genuinely buys you focus or capabilities you don't have – not as a hiding place for problems you don't want to face.

Topic: .... Date: ....

Build Cadence – a Rhythm You Can Rely On

If nobody trusts the build, all your planning is theory.
Only making builds "when someone screams" is a good way to hide problems until it's too late.
Build cadence is simply the rhythm at which you produce usable builds of the game – for yourself, for the team, for tests, for partners. The goal is not "as often as possible". The goal is a rhythm that fits your current phase, your tools and your people, and that you can sustain without destroying development.
You want a plan you decide on ahead of time, then adjust deliberately when reality changes – not a random pattern driven only by emergencies.

What a healthy build cadence does

A healthy cadence:

- Makes it normal to see the real game regularly, not only in screenshots and branches.
- Gives you known moments for testing, feedback and reviews, instead of chaotic "can someone make a build today?".
- Surfaces integration problems early – broken features, content conflicts, performance issues – while they are still cheap to fix.
- Respects the fact that every build has a cost: integrations, hotfixes, context switches for the team.

The right frequency depends on your project size, phase, tools and stability. A small team in pre-production can live with a rough, frequent build. A big production team might aim for fewer but more reliable builds. There is no one magic number – but "no plan" is always the wrong answer.

Choosing a rhythm that fits your project

Instead of chasing an abstract ideal, start with a few practical questions:

- Purpose: what do you need builds for right now – internal playtests, design reviews, QA, partner checks, performance profiling, something else?
- Stability: how stable is your project and toolchain? Does each build require lots of manual fixing, or is it mostly automated?
- Phase: are you exploring (pre-prod), scaling up (production), locking down (beta), or operating (live)? Different phases need different rhythms.
- Capacity: how much time do builds currently eat – and who pays that cost (programmers, integrators, QA)?

From there, you can agree on a simple baseline like "we aim for at least one solid internal build every X days" and add extra builds on top when there is a clear reason. The important part is that you decide the baseline together, instead of pretending you can always "just build" with no impact.
Be honest: builds that are too rare mean you find out about integration problems late. Builds that are too frequent, with heavy manual work each time, will quietly eat your development time.

Try this

On the right page, use these questions to design a build cadence for the next few months of your project:

1. Who actually needs builds, and why?

List the main groups (core team, QA, stakeholders, partners) and what each of them needs builds for.

2. How stable do builds need to be for each use?

Can some audiences handle rough builds, while others only see more stable ones?

3. Given your current phase and tools, what is a realistic baseline?

Write one sentence:
"For the next stage we aim for a build that the team can play every ..."

4. What will you stop doing if builds start consuming too much time?

Note in advance what you will simplify, automate or drop if build work begins to dominate.

5. How will you know the cadence is wrong?

Write down 2–3 concrete signals (for example: "we keep cancelling playtests", "we spend more time fixing builds than adding value") that tell you it's time to adjust the rhythm.

Review this page whenever your phase changes or your tools improve. Your cadence should evolve with the project – but always as a choice, not as a reaction to the latest fire.

Watch out

A build system that only kicks in "on demand" trains everyone to fear builds and to delay integration until the last moment. On the other hand, a cadence that tries to pump out "show builds" all the time can trap the team in a loop of quick fixes and last-minute scrambles, with little space left for real progress. The point of setting a cadence is simple: make builds predictable, trustworthy and affordable, so they help you see the truth about the game instead of becoming yet another source of chaos.

Topic: .... Date: ....

Internal Deadlines vs External Dates

If you treat an external date as your real last day, you're planning to miss it.
Internal deadlines are not fake. They're what keeps external dates from blowing up.
An external date is any commitment that exists outside your team: platform submissions, certification windows, publisher milestones, marketing beats, events, launch windows, contracts. These dates usually have consequences if you slip: lost opportunities, penalties, broken trust.
An internal deadline is a date you set for yourselves: "we want this build ready by...", "we lock content by...", "we freeze code by...". These exist to give you decision points, breathing room and time to fix things before you hit the external wall.

What external dates are really for
External dates are promises to people who are not in your daily stand-ups. They coordinate your game with:

- platform processes and store slots,
- partner expectations and contracts,
- marketing activities and visibility windows,
- other titles in your own portfolio.

You don't control all of them, and changing them is often expensive or politically painful. That's why they should be treated as hard edges in your plan, not flexible suggestions.

What internal deadlines are for
Internal deadlines are tools, not decorations on a roadmap.
They are there to:

- create earlier checkpoints where you can see if you're on track,
- protect time to react – fix blockers, polish, cut scope deliberately,
- sync the team around a realistic "ready by" date that is not the last possible moment.

An internal deadline that always moves "just a bit later" because it's "only internal" is not doing its job. It stops being a tool and becomes background noise.

Linking them: simple rule
A healthy project keeps a clear gap between the two:

- External date = when the outside world expects something from you.
- Internal deadline = when you want to have it ready in a state you're not ashamed of.

The simple rule:
"For every important external date, set at least one earlier internal deadline that gives you time to fix, cut, or adjust."
You don't need complex math. You do need to be honest: if your internal date is only one or two days before a major external commitment, it is not a buffer – it is wishful thinking.

Try this
On the right page, take your current project and walk through these questions:

1. What are our next 3–5 external dates?

Write them down with a short label: certification, partner review, trailer, launch window, event, whatever applies.

2. For each external date, what is our internal "ready" moment?

Note when you expect the team to realistically have the build, assets or material in a usable state – not perfect, but solid.

3. Is there real space between them?

For each pair, write one sentence:
"What will we use the time between internal and external for?"
If the honest answer is "nothing, we're planning to be done at the last moment", admit it.

4. What moves if we see we're not going to hit an internal date?

Write down which levers you will pull first: reduce scope, move work to later, add a small tech/content pass, renegotiate externally if truly needed.
If you find external dates with no internal counterpart, or pairs with no real gap, mark them. Those are the places where you are currently hoping, not planning.

Watch out
Treating external dates as if they were your real last day forces all problems into the final stretch, where every decision is more expensive and more emotional. Treating internal deadlines as optional ("it's just internal, we can slide it") slowly teaches the team that no date means anything until someone panics. And assuming that external partners or platforms will always "understand" and move things for you is a fast way to lose credibility. The job of production here is simple: make external dates visible, create internal deadlines that sit meaningfully in front of them, and respect those internal markers enough that you see trouble early, while you still have room to act.

Topic: .... Date: ....

Cutting Features Without Drama

Cutting features is not failure. Refusing to cut when you should is.
Every project starts with more ideas than time, people and budget. If you never cut, scope will cut you later – in quality, stability, or team sanity. The goal is not to protect every idea. The goal is to protect the game, the core loop, and what makes it worth playing.
Cutting is a normal production tool. The more normal and rule-based you make it, the less drama you get.

Clear criteria beat feelings
When deciding what to cut, start from the game, not from who suggested the idea.

Use simple criteria like:
- Does it support our USP and pillars? If it doesn't show what makes this game special, it's a candidate to go.
- Does it strengthen the core loop? If the feature is far from what players do most of the time, it's easier to cut.
- What is cost vs value? Long, risky implementation for a small, niche benefit is hard to justify.
- What happens if we don't ship it? If the game is still clear, fun and honest without it, you can survive without it.

You don't need a scoring system, but an honest conversation using the same criteria every time.

How to talk about cuts with the team
Cutting hurts most when it feels random or personal. Your job is to make it impersonal and traceable:
- Start from the constraints and goals, not from the feature. "Given our time, budget and dates, we have to make space."
- Tie the decision back to pillars and core loop. "We keep what best serves this experience we're trying to deliver."
- Be specific about what exactly is cut and what is kept. Sometimes you can keep a smaller version or a hook for later.
- Acknowledge the work and emotion already invested. People don't need a speech; they need to know you see their effort.

It's fine to have a "not for this version" parking lot. Moving something there is different from pretending it will magically fit now. Be honest about the fact that many parked ideas will never return – and that this is normal.

Try this
On the right page, pick 3–5 features or ideas from your current project that are causing tension around scope or time.
For each one, write:
1. One sentence on how (if at all) it supports your USP and pillars.
2. One sentence on how it touches or doesn't touch the core loop.
3. One line on the realistic cost: time, people, risks.
4. One clear verdict for this version: keep as is / shrink / move to "later" / cut.

Then look at the whole list and ask yourself:
- "If we cut or shrink these, does the game get worse, or does it get sharper?"

If the game feels sharper and more focused, you're cutting in the right direction.

Watch out
The worst cuts are the ones robbing the game of its USP: you keep all the safe, familiar bits and quietly kill the thing that made it different. Almost as bad are panic cuts at the end, made in a rush, without checking how they affect the core loop or player understanding. And somewhere in the middle sits silent non-cutting: nobody dares to say no, everything stays on paper, and the team just works longer and harder trying to fit an impossible puzzle.
Cutting features without drama means you decide early, explain clearly, and protect the heart of the game instead of its longest wish list.

Topic: .... Date: ....

Block C
Production & Processes

Topic: ....

Date: ....

Work Model: Agile-ish in Gamedev

Most game teams don't run "pure Scrum" or "pure Kanban". They run whatever half-works, plus a lot of habits nobody ever wrote down. That's fine – as long as you know what your model is and keep adjusting it on purpose, not by accident.
Your work model is simply: how work moves through the team, who decides what's next, and how often you stop to look at the game and change course. If you don't choose it, you still have one – it's just invisible and usually messy.

Scrum, Kanban, Hybrid – in practice

You can google the theory. Here's the short, practical view:

- Scrum-ish in gamedev usually means: fixed-length sprints, some form of planning and review, maybe a retro. It works better when you have a relatively stable backlog for the next 1–2 sprints and clear sprint goals. It breaks when every priority changes mid-week and you pretend it doesn't.
- Kanban-ish usually means: continuous flow, no hard sprint box, focus on WIP and keeping the board moving. It works better when work arrives unpredictably (live ops, support, lots of bugfixes) and you care about throughput. It breaks when "no WIP limits" turns into "everyone does a bit of everything forever".
- Hybrid is what most teams actually do: planning by chunks (iterations, milestones) plus a flowing board and a few regular ceremonies. The point is not to impress anyone with vocabulary but to match phase, team size and chaos level.

If "we're agile" means "we change priorities daily with no explanation, no board and no plan", that's not agility. That's noise.

Choose a model that fits your game now
Instead of asking "which framework is right?", ask:

- What phase are we in – exploring, scaling, locking, or live?
- How often does our priority stack realistically change – daily, weekly, monthly?
- How many people need to coordinate across disciplines for a typical feature?
- How often do we need to see the game together and decide: keep, change, cut?

You can then make simple, honest choices:

- How often you plan (weekly, bi-weekly, per milestone).
- How often you review builds together.
- Who owns the board and keeps it reflecting reality.
- How you limit WIP so things actually finish.

Write this down in a few lines. That's your current work model. You can change it later – but change it explicitly, not because it slowly fell apart.

Try this
On the right page, describe how you actually want work to flow for the next few months:

1. Write one sentence: "Our team mostly works like [Scrum-ish / Kanban-ish / Hybrid] because...".
2. Define your planning rhythm: how often you choose goals and pull new work.
3. Define your review rhythm: how often you look at a build together and decide what it changes.
4. Note who is the decision owner for priorities when there's a conflict.
5. List 2 things in your current way of working that clearly help, and 2 that clearly hurt.

Look at what you wrote and ask: "Is this how we actually work, or how we pretend we work?" If there's a gap, that's your first improvement task.

Watch out
Copy-pasting ceremonies from a blog post without understanding why you need them. Calling chaos "agile" to justify constant reprioritisation with no explanation. Keeping a beautiful board that nobody uses while real work happens in DMs and side chats. The model itself doesn't ship the game – but when it's invisible or dishonest, it quietly makes everything harder than it has to be.

Topic: .... Date: ....

Sprint Planning Basics – Steps, Pitfalls

A sprint plan that ignores capacity is not a plan, it's a wish list.
Sprint planning is not "throw tasks into the board until it looks full". It's a short conversation where you decide, together, what you will actually try to finish in the next 1–2 weeks – and what you won't.
Done well, sprint planning connects three things:

- what matters most right now (priorities),
- what is realistically possible (capacity, risks, dependencies),
- what "finished enough" means for this sprint (acceptance).

Before you enter the room

Going into sprint planning with zero prep guarantees noise. Before the meeting, someone (usually producer / lead) should have at least:

- a current priority view – which features, fixes or areas matter most for the next sprint, based on your roadmap and reality,
- a rough sense of capacity – who is available, any holidays, other commitments,
- known dependencies and builds – what is blocked, what must be ready for any upcoming reviews or external dates.

You don't need perfect data. You do need enough to avoid planning in a vacuum.

The basic sequence

In the meeting, keep the flow simple and visible:

1. Set the sprint goal

One or two clear sentences: what you want to achieve by the end of this sprint. Not a list of tickets – a short description of outcome or focus.

2. Select the work that serves that goal

Pull items from your backlog or board that directly support the goal: features, content, tech tasks, bugfixes. If something doesn't support the goal, think twice before pulling it in.

3. Sanity-check capacity and risk

Look at how much you just pulled vs who is available. Call out obvious risks: tricky work, new systems, external dependencies. If it already looks too much, it is.

4. Clarify what "done" means for this sprint

For the most important items, make sure everyone shares the same definition of done at sprint level: implemented, integrated, testable, visible in the build – whatever "finished enough" means now.

5. Confirm commitments

Ask, not rhetorically: "Given what we know, does this look doable?" Adjust. It's better to cut now than pretend you will magically fit three extra days into the sprint later.

The result you want is simple: a short list of sprint goals and items that the team believes in, not silently laughs at.

Try this

On the right page, take a hard look at how you currently plan sprints:

1. Write how sprint planning usually feels in your project in a few words: rushed, chaotic, formal, useful, something else.
2. For your last sprint, reconstruct:
    - What was the real goal (if any)?
    - How much did you actually finish, and why?
3. List three things that regularly go wrong (for example: no clear goal, ignoring capacity, hidden dependencies).
4. Note one or two changes you want to test in the next 2–3 sprint plannings – and after each, quickly jot down whether they helped.

Repeat this exercise a few times. The point is not to run "perfect Scrum". The point is to keep nudging your planning closer to something that reflects reality and serves the game.

Watch out

Planning by who shouts loudest, instead of by goals and priorities. Treating every sprint as a fresh start, with no memory of what you learned from the last one. Filling the board to look productive, then acting surprised when half of it rolls over. And, maybe worst of all, holding sprint planning because "that's what teams do", while nobody in the room can answer the most basic question: "What are we trying to achieve in the next two weeks, and can we actually do it?"

Topic: .... Date: ....

Board Anatomy – To Do / Doing / Review / Done

A pretty board that doesn't match reality is worse than no board at all.
The point of a board is simple: show where the work really is, so everyone can make better decisions. Nothing more magical than that.
You don't need ten columns and a colour system. You need a few clear states that everyone understands the same way, and the discipline to keep them honest.

The minimal flow

Think of your board as a simple story of each piece of work:
Backlog → To Do → Doing → Review → Done

That's enough for most teams, especially if you're not running a huge multi-project machine.

- Backlog – ideas, future work, not committed. Stuff you might do someday, not this week.
- To Do – selected work for the next short horizon (current sprint/iteration), ready to be started. Clear enough that someone can pick it up without a big meeting.
- Doing – things actively worked on right now. Someone is actually moving it forward today, not "maybe soon".
- Review – work that needs another pair of eyes: code review, design check, testing, sign-off. It's not finished, but it's not in active development either.
- Done – finished according to your Definition of Done, not "dev says it's done". Integrated, testable and not waiting on invisible follow-up.

If you want, you can later split columns (for example: "Review" and "Testing" separately) or add simple labels for blocked work. Start from the basics, then expand only when you feel real pain your current columns can't express.

WIP is about finishing, not policing

You don't need complex work-in-progress rules. Just understand the idea:
If there are too many items in Doing, nothing finishes fast. People juggle tasks, context-switch, and everything crawls.
A good rule of thumb: if your Doing column looks like a shopping list, you probably need to stop starting new things and push more items all the way to Done.

You don't have to write a number on the board. Just make it normal to ask:

- "Do we really need to start this now, or should we finish something first?"
- "Who is actually moving this ticket today?"

Try this

On the right page, sketch your real board, not the one from the handbook.

1. Draw your current columns and write under each what they actually mean today. Be honest – if "Done" really means "dev done, QA later", write that.
2. Next to it, draw a clean version using the simple flow above: Backlog, To Do, Doing, Review, Done.
3. For each column, note in a few words:
   - what belongs there,
   - what must be true before an item moves on,
   - what you'd like to change compared to today.

Then pick one change you can make in the next week: renaming a column, redefining "Done", or agreeing that "Doing" should contain fewer parallel items. Try it, observe what happens, adjust.

Watch out

Boards that are always outdated because nobody feels responsible for them. Columns used as decoration only, while real work and decisions live in private chats and side documents. A "Done" column that quietly hides all the unfinished follow-up work: no test, no integration, no polish, no communication. And boards so complicated that people stop looking at them altogether. A simple, honest board with five clear states will do more for your project than any perfect template you're too busy to maintain.

Topic: .... Date: ....

Daily Stand-up Cheatsheet – Questions that Matter

If your daily stand-up regularly takes 30 minutes and solves nothing, it's not a stand-up – it's a slow meeting.
The point is simple: keep work flowing, surface blockers early, and sync just enough so people know what's going on. Nothing more.
You're not there to perform status for the producer, but to help each other finish things.

What the stand-up is actually for

A good daily stand-up does three things:

- Makes it clear what is moving toward Done today.
- Exposes blockers and risks early, before they explode.
- Aligns people on who needs to talk to whom after the stand-up.

That's it. Design debates, deep planning and long problem-solving belong after the stand-up, in smaller groups.
Keep it short, focused and boring in a good way.

Questions that keep it useful

The classic "What did you do yesterday / today / blockers?" is fine – until everyone starts reciting a script and nobody listens.
Try centering on flow instead. For each person (or for each key item on the board), use questions like:

- "Which task are you moving closer to Done today?"
- "What might block you or others today?"
- "Do you need anything from someone here after this call?"

You can still mention "yesterday" if it matters, but the focus is forward: what changes in the next 24 hours.
If things get detailed, park them: "Let's take this right after stand-up – you, you and me."

Try this

On the right page, do a quick reality check on your current stand-ups:

1. Describe in a few words how they feel right now: fast, slow, useful, pointless, something in between.
2. Think of the last week and note:
   - How often did stand-up unblock something?
   - How often did it turn into a long design or tech discussion?
   - How often did people just report to one person instead of talking to each other?
3. Write down one small change you want to test for the next 5 stand-ups. For example:
   - using the "What are you moving to Done today?" question,
   - standing near the board and talking about tickets, not vague tasks,
   - hard stop at 10–15 minutes and parking anything deeper.
4. After those 5 stand-ups, come back to this page and add a short note:
   - "What got better?"
   - "What stayed annoying?"
   - "What one thing will we keep from now on?"

Don't redesign the whole ritual at once. Nudge it, observe, adjust.

Watch out

Stand-ups that regularly morph into long problem-solving sessions. Ten people standing around while two argue about implementation details. Meetings where everyone talks to the producer instead of to the team, like a daily exam. People arriving unprepared, mumbling generic updates that help no one: "same as yesterday, still working on stuff".
Daily stand-up is a sharp tool if you treat it as such: short, concrete, focused on keeping work moving and on making blockers visible. Everything else can – and should – happen somewhere else.

Topic: .... Date: ....

Backlog Grooming – How Often, With Whom, What to Look At

If you never groom the backlog, it becomes a graveyard.
If you groom it badly, it becomes a lie.
Grooming (refinement) is not about rewriting the whole plan every week. It's about keeping future work clear, small enough and honest, so sprint planning and day-to-day decisions don't turn into chaos. Done regularly and lightly, it saves you hours of confusion later.
You want a regular cadence that fits your team – for many teams that's about once per week or once per iteration – and a small group of people who take this seriously instead of treating it as optional admin.

What grooming is (and isn't)

Grooming is:

- making upcoming work clearer: better titles, a bit of context, simple acceptance criteria;
- breaking big blobs into smaller, more workable pieces;
- removing or parking things you know you won't do;
- checking that top items still match current priorities.

Grooming is not:

- re-designing half the game live in the meeting;
- re-prioritising the entire backlog every time;
- inviting the whole team to argue about every ticket;
- doing sprint planning in disguise.

Think of it as cleaning your workbench: enough that you can find the tools you need, not a full remodel every time.

How often and with whom

The exact frequency is less important than having a fixed rhythm and sticking to it. "We groom the backlog regularly" should mean something concrete on your calendar, not "when we remember".
A simple pattern that works for many teams:

- short, regular session (for example, 30–60 minutes) at a predictable time;
- producer or whoever owns the board;
- relevant leads or senior people for upcoming work (design, code, art, etc.);
- occasionally, individual contributors invited when their specific area is being shaped.

You don't need a huge group. You need enough brains in the room to avoid making bad assumptions.

What to look at during grooming

Keep it practical. For the next few sprints or weeks of work:

- Trim: close or park items that clearly won't happen, duplicates, outdated ideas. It's better to admit "not for this project" than to pretend everything is still alive.
- Clarify: for the most important upcoming items, make sure they have a clear title, a short description, and a simple "this will be done when..." note.
- Slice: break down things that are obviously too big to fit into a single sprint or to be owned by one person.
- Check alignment: glance at the top of the backlog – does it still reflect your current goals, or is old stuff sitting above more important new work?

Stop when you have enough ready work for the next planning, not when the backlog looks perfect.

Try this

On the right page, design grooming for your current project:

1. Write how often you realistically want to groom (weekly, every sprint, other).
2. Note who should always be there, and who should be invited only when needed.
3. Describe in a few lines what "good enough for next sprint" means for your tickets (clarity, size, acceptance).
4. Think back to the last month and list the main symptoms of bad grooming you've seen: messy tickets, surprises in planning, dead ideas clogging the top. Next to each, write one small rule you will try (for example: "if a ticket is untouched for 3 months, we park it").

Use this page a few times as your grooming evolves, adjusting frequency and attendees as reality teaches you what works.

Watch out

Never grooming at all and then wondering why planning is painful and everything takes longer than expected. Turning every grooming session into a full design workshop where you argue about features instead of preparing work. Re-prioritising the entire backlog every time so nobody trusts the order anymore. And treating the backlog as sacred, where nothing is ever removed – even when everyone knows half of it will never happen. A light, honest grooming habit beats any perfect process you're too busy to follow.

Topic: .... Date: ....

Bug Triage – Priority Criteria & Workflow

If every bug is top priority, nothing is.
Triage is not about winning arguments between QA and devs. It's a simple way to decide what gets fixed now, what waits, and what may never be fixed – based on impact and timing, not volume or drama.
You don't need a huge taxonomy. You need a shared language and a routine that the producer can run without starting a war every time.

Severity vs Priority – don't mix them up
Start with two separate ideas:

- Severity – how bad is it when it happens?

Think in terms of player impact: crash, progression block, broken core loop vs cosmetic annoyance.

- Priority – when do we deal with it?

This depends on where you are in the project, what you're trying to ship next, and how much capacity you have.
You can call your levels whatever you like. A simple example that most teams understand:

- **Critical** – crashes, hard locks, data loss, progression blockers, broken builds.
- **Major** – significant issues in core gameplay or UX; ugly but survivable problems in key flows.
- **Minor** – cosmetic issues, low-impact edge cases, small annoyances that don't break play.

Rename or add levels if you need to – the important part is that everyone uses them the same way.
Priority then answers: "Given our next milestone, which of these do we actually fix now?" A Critical bug is almost always high priority. A Minor bug can sometimes become high priority if it affects a key partner build or a critical first-time user experience. Context matters.

A minimal triage workflow
Keep the workflow lightweight and regular:

1. **Report**

Someone finds a bug and logs it with a clear title, repro steps, expected vs actual behaviour, and build info. Messy reports waste time.

2. **Reproduce**

Confirm you can see it. If it's not reproducible, mark it as such but don't just throw it away – note conditions and keep an eye out.

3. **Classify**

Assign severity based on impact and give it a draft priority based on current goals. This is where producer and leads often step in.

4. **Assign**

Decide who will handle it, or explicitly mark it as "won't fix" or "later". "Someone will pick it up" usually means nobody will.

5. **Verify**

Once it's marked fixed, someone (often QA) re-tests on a relevant build and only then closes it. This is how you avoid regressions quietly piling up.

Triage works best on a steady rhythm: short, regular sessions where you look at new and reopened bugs, adjust priorities, and check the top of the list against your next milestone.

Try this
On the right page, design bug triage for your current project:

1. Write down the severity levels you want to use (you can start from Critical / Major / Minor) and give each one a one-line description in plain language.
2. Describe, in a few sentences, how you will set priority: who decides, how often you review, and how upcoming milestones influence the order.
3. Sketch your triage rhythm: how often you meet, who joins, and what you want to leave each triage session with (for example: "top N bugs confirmed and assigned").
4. Note how you will handle regressions and "won't fix" decisions so they don't disappear silently.

Revisit this page after a couple of intense weeks and adjust your rules based on what actually happened.

Watch out
Treating all bugs as equally urgent and then wondering why nothing important ever really gets finished. Ignoring regressions or reopening bugs because "we don't have time" – until players or partners find them in the worst possible moment. And closing bugs without verification, using the tracker as a comfort blanket instead of a reflection of reality. A small, honest triage routine with clear severity, realistic priorities and a closed verification loop will save you more pain than any huge, perfect bug process that nobody respects.

Topic: .... Date: ....

Build Review Template – What to Look At Each Time

If you never actually play your builds, you're managing a slide deck, not a game.
A build review doesn't need a 10-page report. It needs a short, repeatable checklist that forces you to look at the right things and write down a few honest notes.
As a producer, your goal is simple: every time a "notable build" appears (end of sprint, before sharing with others), someone actually plays it, looks at key areas, and captures what changed – better, worse, and riskier.

What a light build review should cover

Think in five passes. You don't have to write essays for each; a few lines are enough.

1. Core loop
   - Does the main gameplay still feel as good as last time, or better, or worse?
   - Anything new that confuses or slows down what players do most of the time?
2. New features / content
   - Are the new things actually visible and usable in the build?
   - Do they behave roughly as expected, or are they obviously half-wired?
3. Performance & stability
   - Any new hitches, long loads, obvious drops in frame rate?
   - Crashes or hard locks that appeared with this build?
4. UX & clarity
   - Did the changes make anything clearer or more confusing?
   - Are menus, prompts, feedback still understandable without explanation?
5. Risks & surprises
   - What in this build worries you if you had to ship in a few weeks?
   - What behaviour makes you think "this will explode later if we ignore it"?

You can adjust the labels if you want. The important thing is to look at the same few areas every time, so you see trends, not random impressions.

A simple structure for your notes

Your build review can fit on half a page. For each notable build, capture:

- Build info – date, label/branch, what this build is for (internal review, partner, test).
- Highlights – a few lines on what's clearly better than last time.
- Issues – the most painful regressions or new problems you noticed.
- Risks / questions – things you're not sure about yet but that smell dangerous.
- Follow-ups – 3–5 specific actions or checks you want the team to do next.

That's it. No one is going to read a novel after every build. But almost everyone can understand one compact page with clear highlights and follow-ups.

Try this

On the right page, draft your own minimal build review template for the current project.

1. At the top, reserve space for Date / Build label / Purpose.
2. Create 3–5 short sections you commit to filling every time (for example: Core loop, New stuff, Performance & stability, UX, Risks & follow-ups).
3. Under each section, write one guiding question that will push you to be honest, like "What feels worse than in the previous build?" or "What in this build would I be afraid to show to a partner?"

Use this template for the next few important builds and adjust it after you've filled it a couple of times. If a section stays empty every time, either you don't need it, or you're not really looking.

Watch out

Only reading changelogs and never actually playing the game. Treating build reviews as a performance where people defend their work, instead of a chance to see reality together. Writing huge review documents that nobody has time to read or act on. And, maybe the most common: doing informal "quick looks" at builds but never writing down what you saw, so the same problems surprise you again two weeks later. A small, consistent review template beats any sophisticated process you're too busy to use.

Topic: .... Date: ....

Internal Release Checklist (Internal Build)

If you're not willing to run the build yourself for a few minutes, don't send it to anyone else.
An internal release should not be perfect – but it should be intentionally good enough for the people who will touch it.
"Internal build" can mean different things: something for the wider team to play, a QA drop, a partner preview, a focus review. The exact checklist changes with the audience and purpose, but the idea is the same: no surprises you already knew about and could have avoided.

What "internal release" means here

On this page, "internal release" means any build that leaves the immediate dev bubble and goes to:

- the wider team, QA or support, other teams in the company, trusted partners or stakeholders seeing a non-public build.

This is stricter than "I hit Play in the editor", but looser than a full platform submission. It's your minimum professional bar.

Minimum gates before you hit Send

As producer, you don't have to personally click every button – but you own the bar. For most internal releases, the basics should be:

- The build compiles and boots cleanly on the target platform without manual hacks.
- A short smoke test has been done: you can start a new game or load a save, play a few minutes, and exit without obvious disasters.
- The main flow you want people to see (test area, new feature, key level) actually works well enough to be tried.
- There is a small known issues note: things you already know are broken, so testers and stakeholders don't waste time rediscovering them.

For some audiences (QA, tech-heavy reviews), you can live with rougher edges. For non-technical people, you probably want a little more stability and clarity. Adjust the strictness, not the honesty.

Adjusting to audience and purpose

Before releasing, ask three simple questions:

- Who is this build for? Wider team, QA, partner, execs?
- What do we want them to do with it? Playtest, break it, approve a feature, give a go/no-go?
- What must work for them to do that? Specific menu, level, feature, control scheme?

Your checklist then changes shape:

- For QA: focus on reproducibility, debug info, and access to areas under test.
- For designers / team playtests: smoother UX, clear entry points, cheats or shortcuts explained.
- For stakeholders or partners: the path you want them on should be solid, even if other parts are rough.

Write this down once, so "QA drop" and "playtest build" don't secretly mean different things to each person.

Communication that travels with the build

A good internal release is half build, half message. Every time you send one, there should be a small, consistent note:

- what this build is for, what's new or changed since the last one, where you want people to focus, how to report issues or feedback (tool, channel, tag).

Without that, you get random testing, repeated bug reports, and lots of "is this supposed to be broken?" noise.

Try this

On the right page, sketch your own internal release checklist.

1. First, list the main types of internal builds you send (for example: QA drop, team playtest, partner preview).
2. For each type, write 3–5 short bullets:
   - what absolutely must be true before you send it,
   - what you're okay with being rough or broken,
   - what info must go into the release note.
3. Add one final line for yourself: "If I had to show this build personally to someone important, would I be embarrassed?" If the answer is yes, refine the checklist.

Use and tweak this page as you ship a few internal builds. The goal is not zero bugs – the goal is that nobody in your team is surprised by avoidable ones.

Watch out

"Surprise builds" appearing in people's inboxes with no context, no notes and no idea what to look at. Sending obviously broken builds to QA or stakeholders and pretending it's fine because "it's only internal". Sharing drops with dev cheats, debug overlays and god-mode left on without telling anyone. And assuming that the build itself will speak for you, when a two-paragraph release note could have saved hours of confusion.

Topic: .... Date: ....

Working with QA – What to Give, What to Expect

QA is not here to clean up after you. They are here to help you see the truth about the game.
On a day-to-day basis, in-house QA is one of your closest partners in production. They sit right where gameplay, tech and player experience meet. If you treat QA as a dumping ground for messy builds or as "police", you waste one of the most powerful tools you have.
Your job is to make sure collaboration is clear: what you give QA, what you expect back, and how that loop runs every day.

What QA needs from you

QA can't test intentions. They test what's actually in the build. To do that well, they need more than "here's the exe":

- A build they can actually use
- Not perfect, but stable enough to launch, navigate and reach the areas you care about without constant hard locks.
- Context and focus
- A short note for each drop: what changed, what's risky, what you'd like them to focus on, what they can ignore for now.
- Basic documentation of flows
- How to reach new features, hidden menus, dev shortcuts. QA shouldn't be guessing secret inputs from Slack screenshots.
- Decent bug intake
- When the dev team logs issues, they should include clear titles, repro steps, build numbers and expected vs actual behaviour. Vague tickets slow everyone down.
- Two-way communication channels
- A known place and format for questions: "Is this intended?", "How should we treat this area?", "What's the current priority?"

If QA has to reverse-engineer every build and decision, you will get shallow coverage and a lot of frustration.

What you can expect from QA

In return, it's fair to expect QA to be more than a list of random bugs.
From a functioning QA partnership you should see:

- Clear, actionable reports

Bugs that can be reproduced, understood and prioritised. Screens, logs or videos when they actually help, not for show.

- Trends, not just tickets

Signals like: "crashes are spiking in this area", "new feature X keeps confusing first-time players", "performance on platform Y is degrading".

- Risk flags

Honest warnings when a build is too unstable for wider use, or when a particular area looks dangerous for an upcoming milestone, cert or event.

- Support in decision-making

Data and examples that help you decide what to fix now, what to park, and where to focus limited time before a key date.

QA's role is not to shout "broken" at everything. It's to help you aim limited attention where it will matter most.

Try this

On the right page, sketch how you want to work with QA on your current project.

1. Write, in a few lines, what you will give QA with each build: level of stability, minimum smoke test, short notes, focus areas. Be honest about what you can do consistently.
2. Write what you expect from QA in return: how they report bugs, how often they summarise trends, how they raise urgent risks.
3. Note the channels you'll use together: where build notes go, where urgent issues are raised, where questions are asked (and answered).
4. Think back over the last month and list the biggest pain points with QA collaboration: messy builds, ignored feedback, bad bug reports, something else. Next to each pain point, write one small change you can test in the next few weeks.

Revisit this page after a release or a busy period and adjust the rules based on what actually helped.

Watch out

Treating QA as a trash bin: throwing them unstable builds with no notes and then complaining that the reports are noisy. Ignoring QA feedback until the same issues show up in front of players, partners or platform holders. Accepting terrible bug reports from the dev side – no repro, no context, no build info – and quietly expecting QA to guess what's going on. Working with QA every day means making the loop explicit: we give you enough to do your job, you give us enough clarity to do ours, and we both tell the truth about where the game is really at.

Topic: .... Date: ....

Production Risk Log – Micro Format

If you don't write risks down, you're not managing them – you're just hoping.
Back in Risk Overview at the Start you looked at big risks at project kick-off. This page is about the day-to-day version of that: a tiny, living risk log you can actually keep up to date while the project moves.
You don't need a monster spreadsheet with fifty columns. For most game teams, a short list of the top few risks, reviewed regularly, is enough to change decisions. The bigger the project and organisation, the more factors you'll consider – but the core idea stays the same.

Risk vs Issue – quick reminder

- A risk is something that might happen and would hurt you if it does: missed date, key person leaving, tech not scaling, platform change, rating problem, whatever fits your project.
- An issue is already happening: the person has left, the build is broken, the cert was rejected.

The risk log is about risks: problems you can still influence before they bite.

A micro format that fits on one page

At this level, you only need five pieces of information per risk:

- Risk – a short, concrete description: "Save system won't handle our final content size", "Key console port vendor may slip", "Team burns out before launch".
- Likelihood – rough feel: low / medium / high.
- Impact – if it happens: annoying / painful / catastrophic.
- Owner – one person who watches this risk and chases updates.
- Next check – when you'll explicitly look at it again.
-

That's all. No scoring matrix, no formulas. Just enough to point your attention and to avoid the classic "we all knew it was a risk but nobody really owned it".
In a tiny team, this might be 3–5 lines on one page. In a larger project, you might track more, or split by area (production, tech, content, external).

How to keep it alive

A risk log is useful only if you touch it regularly. As producer or lead, set a simple rhythm:

- glance at it before key meetings (planning, milestone reviews),
- update likelihood/impact when reality changes,
- close risks that have clearly passed,
- add new ones when you feel that "this could really hurt us later" itch.

You're not trying to predict everything. You're trying to avoid being surprised by things you already suspected.

Try this

On the right page, start – or refresh – your own micro risk log for the current project.

1. Write a short heading: project name and "Top Risks – [month/year]".
2. List 3–5 real risks you're worried about right now. For each one, note:
    - the risk (one clear sentence),
    - your rough likelihood and impact,
    - the owner,
    - the next date you'll check it.
3. Add one more line at the bottom:

"When and where will I review this list?" – sprint planning, milestone review, a quick weekly check-in, something else.
Come back to this page every few weeks. Cross out closed risks, adjust others, add new ones. If the page gets too messy, copy the current active ones onto a fresh page and keep going.

Watch out

Gigantic risk registers that look impressive but nobody ever reads or updates. Treating risks as a formality for a slide deck, instead of as a tool to steer scope, dates and focus. Waiting until a risk turns into a full-blown issue before anyone feels "allowed" to act. A small, honest list of the few things that can really hurt your project – and one person clearly owning each – will do more for you than any perfectly structured risk matrix buried in a forgotten folder.

Topic: .... Date: ....

Dependencies Map – Connecting Design, Art, Code, Audio

If you don't see your dependencies, you only notice them when someone is already blocked.
Every meaningful feature in a game is a chain: ***idea → design → tools → assets → implementation → integration → QA → polish***. If you pretend it's just "one ticket", you will keep discovering late that one team is waiting on another, or that you booked work in the wrong order.
This page is about drawing that chain on purpose, so you can schedule work and spot trouble before it quietly burns weeks.

What a dependency really is
A dependency is simply:
"For X to move, Y needs to exist or be decided."
Typical examples:

- Design needs some answers from product/creative before they can lock a feature.
- Art needs design specs and tools before producing assets.
- Code needs final asset formats and APIs before wiring things up.
- Audio needs timings, events and hooks before creating and implementing sound.
- QA needs stable builds and test paths before they can validate anything.

None of this is exotic. The problem is when it's only in people's heads, not on paper.

A simple chain for one feature
For a single feature, you can often sketch a basic chain like:
Feature idea → Design spec → Tooling / tech prep → Content (art/audio/narrative) → Implementation → Integration into builds → QA & iteration
You don't need to capture every micro-step. You need to capture the order in which disciplines depend on each other.
Two key questions for each step:

- "What must exist before this can start?"
- "Who will be stuck if this step slips?"

If you can't answer those, you're already scheduling blind.

Using dependency maps in planning
When you plan a milestone or a big feature:

- Start with the end: what do you want to be testable in a build?
- Work backwards through the chain: what design, tools, assets, code, audio and QA are needed?
- Mark steps that are obviously serial (cannot overlap) vs ones that can move in parallel.
- Spot where the same person or team is a bottleneck for multiple chains.

You're not trying to predict every detail. You're trying to avoid starting a bunch of work that cannot finish because upstream pieces don't exist.

Try this
On the right page, map dependencies for one real feature or slice of your current project:

1. Write the feature/slice name at the top.
2. In a horizontal line, write the key steps from idea to "in build and tested" – only the big ones.
3. Under each step, note:
    - what needs to be decided or delivered before it can start,
    - which discipline / person owns it,
    - who is blocked if it slips.

Then look at your chain and ask:

- "Where are we most likely to get stuck?"
- "Are we currently scheduling anything that clearly depends on things that don't exist yet?"

Use a different colour or simple marks to highlight your top 2–3 risky links.

Watch out
Starting implementation while design is still changing every day, then acting surprised when half the work is rework. Asking art or audio to "just start" without tools, formats or specs, and then blaming them when things don't plug in. Piling features onto a single tech or design owner without noticing that half the project now depends on their week. Dependencies don't disappear if you ignore them – they just ambush you later, when moving dates and scope is much more painful. A simple, honest map for the most important pieces of work will already put you ahead of most teams.

Topic: .... Date: ....

Asset Pipelines – From Concept to Integration

If your asset pipeline lives only in people's heads, you don't have a pipeline – you have a sequence of surprises.
Every asset – 2D, 3D, audio, narrative – walks a path from idea to "really in the game". When that path is unclear, assets get stuck in "almost ready" folders, arrive at the wrong time, or require three reworks because expectations were never aligned.
Your job is not to make the pipeline fancy. Your job is to make it visible, repeatable and good enough for this project.

The basic stages

For most asset types, the high-level stages look something like this:
Brief → Concept → Approval → Production → Review → Integration → Test

You can rename them, but each step should answer a simple question.

- Brief – what is this asset for, where will it appear, what constraints does it have (style, performance, platform, memory, gameplay needs)?
- Concept – quick visual or audio direction so people agree on what "good" roughly looks like.
- Approval – someone with authority says "this is the direction, go make the real thing".
- Production – building the asset to the agreed spec (art, audio, narrative, etc.).
- Review – check against brief and technical constraints, before it disappears into a folder.
- Integration – hooked into the game, referenced correctly, visible or audible in context.
- Test – QA / team verifies it works where it should, doesn't break performance or UX, and behaves as expected.

You don't need to document every sub-step. You do need to be clear about when one stage is finished and the next can start.

Handoffs: what must be true before moving on

Bugs in asset pipelines often come from fuzzy handoffs. Production starts before concept is aligned. Integration starts before naming or formats are consistent. QA tests assets that are already known to be wrong.

For each stage, you want a minimal "ready for next" definition. Examples:

- From Brief to Concept: someone wrote down context, constraints and references, not just "we need a cool sword".
- From Concept to Approval: at least one option checked against the brief; key stakeholders have actually looked at it.
- From Production to Review: asset respects naming, scale, budget, platform rules, and is in the right folder/place.
- From Review to Integration: owner has signed off on "good enough for now", with known issues documented.
- From Integration to Test: asset is in a build that QA / team can reach without hacks.

Keep this tight and simple. A one-line checklist per step is enough.

Different teams, different depth

A small team might keep this whole flow in one person's head and a few lines in a doc. A larger studio might have different pipelines per asset type, with more detailed gates.
The rule of thumb:

- The bigger the team and the more people touching assets,
- the more important it is to write down the path and handoff rules.

You don't win points for complexity. You win when the right assets appear in the game at the right time, with as little chaos as possible.

Try this

On the right page, map a pipeline for one important asset type in your current project (for example: environment props, characters, UI screens, sound effects).

1. Write the stages you currently use, from "we need it" to "it works in game". Be honest – include messy steps like "send DM to X" if that's how it really works.
2. Under each stage, note what must be true before the asset moves on, and who is supposed to check that.
3. Mark the slowest or most painful step in that pipeline: where assets pile up, bounce back, or die. Next to it, jot down a couple of ideas to reduce friction (clearer brief, fewer approvers, better tools, planned integration windows).

Come back to this page after a milestone and adjust based on the problems you actually saw.

Watch out

Assets that live forever in "concept" because nobody is brave enough to approve anything. Assets marked "done" but never integrated, so the folder looks full while the game looks empty. Steps where no one feels responsible for saying "yes, this is ready for the next stage", so work flows randomly based on who shouts. A simple, written pipeline with clear handoffs is often enough to cut days or weeks of hidden waste from your production.

Topic: .... Date: ....

Content Freeze / Code Freeze – When and Why

A freeze is not a punishment. It's a seatbelt. You only miss it when you crash.
Late in a milestone or before a key build, your biggest risk is not "too little stuff". It's too much change, too late. Freeze is the moment you stop adding and start stabilising on purpose – so you don't discover the real state of the game two hours before a deadline.

What we actually mean by "freeze"

Keep it simple:

- Content freeze – no new levels, assets, quests, systems, UI sections, or design changes. Only fixes and small, targeted polish to what's already in.
- Code freeze – no new systems, no big refactors, no risky changes. Only critical fixes and tightly scoped, low-risk adjustments.

In both cases, the rule is the same: stop widening the surface area, so the team can find and fix what's already there.

You can have one or the other, or both at once, depending on what you're preparing: milestone build, external review, cert, launch.

When freezes make sense

Freezes are tools for moments where stability matters more than adding more stuff:

- end of milestone, when you need a build you can confidently show or judge;
- before important external deliveries (publisher review, platform check, public demo);
- in the run-up to cert and launch, where one badly timed change can cost you a window.

You don't need them all the time. But if you never freeze, you're basically betting that constant change near a deadline won't bite you. It usually does.

Rules and exceptions

A freeze without rules is just a vibe. At minimum, you want to be clear on:

- Scope – which branches, platforms, systems and teams are under freeze, and whether it's content, code, or both.
- Duration – from when to when; even if it's approximate, people need a sense of the horizon.
- Exceptions – what can still change (for example: P1 bug fixes only), and what is absolutely banned.

Exceptions should be rare, explicit and owned. Someone with real responsibility (producer, tech lead, project owner) needs to say "yes, we accept this risk" – not "well, if you think it's fine…".

If you are constantly making exceptions "just this once", you don't have a freeze. You have chaos with extra steps.

Try this

On the right page, define what freeze actually means for your project:

1. Write short definitions for content freeze and code freeze in your context: what stops, what is still allowed, in which branches.
2. For each type of freeze, note:
   - who has the authority to announce it;
   - who has the authority to approve exceptions;
   - which kinds of changes are still allowed (for example: crash fixes, cert compliance, text tweaks).
3. List the situations where you will seriously consider a freeze: specific milestones, external reviews, cert submissions, launch, big events.
4. Add one sentence you will use when you announce it, so everyone hears the same message about scope and reason.

Use this page when you prepare the next big delivery. If you realise you're always announcing freezes but never respecting them, that's a separate problem to write down and fix.

Watch out

Announcing a freeze and then breaking it every day "because this change is really small" – until something breaks in a way you can't fix in time. Calling a freeze but never defining what is actually frozen, so half the team assumes it doesn't apply to them. And avoiding freezes completely because they feel "unfriendly", while your actual friendly gesture is to protect the team from last-minute panic. A clear, short freeze with tough exceptions is kinder than a month of crunch caused by endless late surprises.

Topic: .... Date: ....

Retrospective Template – Keep / Drop / Try / Learn

If your retros never change anything, stop doing them.
A retrospective is not a ceremony where everyone politely lists annoyances and then goes back to work the same way. It's a short, structured moment to look at how you worked in the last sprint or milestone and decide what to keep, what to stop, and what to experiment with – without hunting for a person to blame.
Someone (usually a producer or lead) holds the structure. The whole team brings honest input. The goal is simple: next iteration should be slightly less painful than the last one.

The purpose: improve the system, not the targets

Games are built by systems of people, tools and habits. When something goes wrong, it's almost never just "X did a bad job". It's usually a mix of unclear priorities, missing info, time pressure, weak processes, bad timing.
A good retro:

- looks at specific recent events (not abstract "we're bad at communication"),
- talks about behaviours and patterns, not characters,
- ends with a few concrete changes you will actually try.

If people feel they'll be attacked, they stop telling the truth. When the focus is on the system, not on guilt, you get useful data.

The four quadrants

Use the Keep / Drop / Try / Learn format to keep things sharp:

- Keep – things that worked and you want to protect (for example: a useful meeting format, a build cadence that felt right, a collaboration that unlocked progress).
- Drop – practices, habits or rituals that are not worth the time and energy they consume.
- Try – small experiments you'll run in the next iteration to see if they help (new rule, tweak to a meeting, different way of using the board).
- Learn – insights you want to remember: what surprised you, what you'd approach differently next time, what the last sprint taught you about your team or game.

You don't need equal amounts in each box. Some retros will be heavier on "Drop" and "Try", others on "Keep" and "Learn". That's fine.

How to run it

As the person holding structure:

- Set the scope: "We're talking about last sprint / this milestone / that release".
- Give people a few minutes to jot down notes individually for each quadrant.
- Then go through them together, grouping similar points and discussing briefly where needed.
- At the end, pick 1–3 concrete actions (usually from Drop and Try) and write down who owns each and by when you'll check back.

You don't need to resolve everything on the spot. You do need to leave with a small list of decisions and a shared understanding of what you learned.

Try this

On the right page, run a quick retro on your last sprint or milestone using the four quadrants:

1. Draw four sections: Keep / Drop / Try / Learn.
2. For each, write a few short bullet points based on what actually happened – good and bad. Be specific: name concrete meetings, features, decisions or events.
3. Circle one item in Drop and one in Try that you believe would make the biggest difference if you acted on them. Next to each, note:
   - what exactly you will change,
   - who owns making sure it happens,
   - when you'll look back and see if it helped.

Keep this page somewhere visible for the next iteration. When that one ends, skim it during the next retro: did you actually do what you said? Did it help?

Watch out

Retros that turn into quiet blame sessions where everyone talks around the real problems. Lists of feedback that go straight into a document nobody opens again. Overloading the team with ten "action items" instead of two or three meaningful changes. A retro that doesn't shift behaviour is just another meeting. A simple, honest Keep / Drop / Try / Learn, run regularly, is enough to slowly bend your production in a better direction.

Topic: .... Date: ....

Light Incident Postmortem – Analysing Screw-ups

If you never analyse screw-ups, you're doomed to repeat them.
Incidents happen: a bad build goes out, a milestone is missed, the wrong branch gets shipped, a feature lands in a state nobody is happy with. The point of a light postmortem is not to write a five-page report. It's to pause, understand how it happened, and decide what you'll do differently next time.
You're not looking for a person to blame. You're looking for the combination of decisions, habits and gaps that made the screw-up almost inevitable.

What counts as an incident here

For this notebook, think "project incidents", not only disasters:

- broken internal build that wastes a day of testing,
- missed internal or external date,
- big feature landing far below expectations,
- serious miscommunication that derails a sprint or milestone.

If it hurt the project enough that people complained or had to scramble, it's worth a short postmortem.

A light template you can actually use
Keep it to half a page. Four blocks are enough:

1. What happened

Short, factual description. What went wrong, when, who was affected in broad terms. No drama, no spin.

2. Impact

What did it cost: time, money, trust, morale, opportunity. Internally and, if relevant, externally. Be honest.

3. Root causes

Look past the last person who touched the problem. What in your system made this likely? Examples: unclear ownership, missing checklist, no freeze, wrong assumptions, weak communication, tool limits. Name behaviours and conditions, not villains.

4. What we'll change

1–3 concrete changes you will try: a rule, a checklist, a new habit, a different approval step, a clearer responsibility. Small enough to actually implement in the next sprints.

Names can appear in the story ("X triggered the build"), but blame cannot be the outcome. If the only conclusion is "Y screwed up", you learned nothing useful.

Sharing and using it
A light postmortem is only useful if people see it and it influences future decisions.

- Share it with the people involved and anyone affected.
- Keep it short enough that people actually read it.
- Put it somewhere you'll find before the next similar event (release prep doc, milestone folder, decision log).

The goal is that when a similar situation approaches, someone remembers: "Last time we did this, we got burned because of X. Let's not repeat that."

Try this
On the right page, walk one real screw-up from your current or recent project through this template:

1. Write What happened in 3–5 sentences. Stick to facts: what, when, who was impacted.
2. Describe the Impact in a few lines: which dates moved, who had to work extra, what had to be cut or postponed.
3. List the Root causes as behaviours or conditions, not accusations. Ask yourself:
   - "What made this likely?"
   - "What would have had to be different for this not to happen?"
4. Under What we'll change, choose one or two changes you can realistically introduce in the next 1–2 months. Next to each, write who owns it and when you'll check if it helped.

Keep this page. Before your next big build or milestone, come back to it and ask: "Did we actually change anything after that incident, or are we about to repeat it?"

Watch out
Witch-hunts where the main output is shame, not learning. Postmortems that are written once, archived and never influence a single decision. Analyses that obsess over the last click ("who pressed the button") instead of the system that allowed a dangerous button to exist. A light, honest postmortem that leads to one real change beats a perfect analysis nobody reads and nobody acts on.

Topic: .... Date: ....

Remote / Distributed Teams – Minimum Rules

Remote doesn't break projects. Silent, unstructured remote does.
In a hybrid team – some people in the office, some at home – the risk is simple: information sticks where it was said first. Office people hear decisions in the hallway. Remote people hear about them a week later, if at all. Your minimum rules exist to stop that gap from quietly killing the project.

Three pillars: presence, writing, rhythm
For hybrid work with small time-zone differences, you usually need just three things:

1. Shared presence window

A clear block of time when people can reliably reach each other live. Not "we're all online all day", but:
"Between X and Y we assume people are reachable for calls and quick questions."

2. Written decisions by default

Anything that changes priorities, scope, dates, or responsibilities gets written down where everyone can see it. Not just in someone's memory or a private chat thread.

3. Simple communication rhythm

Regular, predictable moments where the team syncs: stand-ups, weekly summary, short written updates. People should not have to guess when they'll next hear what's going on.
If you get these three right, most remote pain drops sharply.

Written decisions: the real source of truth
In a hybrid setup, spoken decisions disappear fast. You need a habit of turning key moments into a few lines of text:
after important calls or heated discussions, after scope cuts, roadmap changes, or priority flips, after incidents and bigger mistakes, after agreeing to "just do it this way from now on".
The format can be simple:
"Decision: ... Because: ... Applies from: ... Owner: ..."
Where you store it (doc, ticket, channel, decision log) matters less than everyone knowing where to look. The test: if a new team member joins, can they reconstruct the last month's key decisions without asking five different people?

Meetings vs async: choose on purpose
Remote and hybrid teams drift into two extremes: either too many meetings or no shared context at all.
Use live meetings for:
decisions that need fast back-and-forth, sensitive topics where tone matters, complex discussions that would explode in a long text thread.
Use async for:
status updates and progress summaries, documenting decisions and plans, questions that don't need an answer in the next 10 minutes.
The minimum rule: if a meeting leads to a decision, someone writes it up. If an async thread grows long and tense, someone schedules a call.

Try this
On the right page, look at how your current hybrid setup actually works:

1. Write down your current pains: missed information, duplicate conversations, people being left out, too many calls, people "disappearing" for days. Be specific.
2. Note where decisions are made today: stand-ups, private chats, random calls, office conversations. How many of those ever get written down?
3. Now define 3–5 minimum rules for your team. For example:
   - "Core hours are from ... to ... for live questions."
   - "Decisions on priorities/dates/scope are always written in ... by the person who owns them."
   - "We do short written weekly summaries in ... so no one has to chase context."
   - "If something affects more than N people, it goes to the shared channel, not a private DM."

These rules don't need to be perfect. They need to be clear enough that people can follow them and simple enough that they survive busy weeks.

Watch out
Decisions made in private chats or quick office talks and never shared, leaving remote people to guess why priorities changed. Meeting overload where half the team sits on calls all day and still feels lost. People going quiet for days because there is no agreed rhythm for updates and no safe way to say "I'm stuck". Minimum rules for hybrid work are not about control. They're about making sure everyone is playing the same game, with the same information, no matter where they sit.

Topic: .... Date: ....

Build Labels & Versioning – Simple Rules

If your builds are called new_new_final_FIX, you don't have versioning – you have chaos.
The point of versioning is not to impress anyone with a clever scheme. It's to answer three basic questions, every time, for everyone:
What is this build? Where did it come from? Is it newer or older than the one I just ran?

What a build label should tell you at a glance
Keep labels short, predictable and boring. Anyone looking at a list of builds should be able to tell:

- Which game / branch this is from.
- Which platform / target it's for.
- Roughly when it was built.
- What it's for (internal QA, demo, store review, hotfix, etc.).

You don't need all of that in one long string if your tools add some of it automatically, but as a producer you want a consistent pattern. For example:
GAME_SHORT-PLATFORM-BRANCH-DATE-BUILDNR
XY-PC-MAIN-2025-03-12-b03
Or, if you prefer a version-first style:
GAME_SHORT-PLATFORM-vMAJOR.MINOR.PATCH-TAG
XY-PC-v0.5.3-INTERNAL_QA
You can combine both ideas. The important part is consistency and that the team knows how to read it.

Simple versioning: MAJOR.MINOR.PATCH (light)
You don't have to implement full formal semantic versioning. A light version is often enough:

- MAJOR – big changes that break compatibility or mark a major phase (alpha, beta, launch, big expansion).
- MINOR – new features, content, visible improvements.
- PATCH – fixes, small tweaks, performance, minor improvements.

Decide what "MAJOR bump" means for your project (for example: alpha → beta → launch, or big DLCs), and use MINOR/PATCH for the everyday builds between those milestones.
One key rule: whatever you choose, write it down for the team so people don't guess when to bump which number.

The version that players and QA actually see
A label in your build system is one thing. The version visible in-game (or in your launcher) is another – and it matters.
Make sure:

- The game shows a clear version string somewhere obvious (main menu, pause menu, debug overlay).
- That version matches what QA sees in their bug reports and what producers see in their release notes.
- People never have to ask "Which build is this?" after launching the game.

The format can be exactly the same as your build label, or a shorter form that still maps back to it (for example: v0.5.3-b03).

Try this
On the right page, design a simple build and versioning scheme for your current project.

1. Write one short format for your build labels, using only elements you truly need. For example:
2. GAME-PLATFORM-BRANCH-DATE-NR or GAME-PLATFORM-vX.Y.Z-TAG.
3. Under it, explain in one line what each part means, in plain language.
4. Decide how you'll use MAJOR.MINOR.PATCH in this project:
   - When will you bump MAJOR?
   - What counts as a MINOR change?
   - What counts as a PATCH?
5. Define where the in-game version will be shown and in what format. Make sure it can be easily matched to a specific build label.
6. Add one rule for yourself as producer:
   - where you'll log each "notable" build (short note: version, date, purpose, key changes),
   - how you'll ensure everyone uses the same naming from now on.

You can refine the scheme later. Start with something simple that the whole team can remember.

Watch out
Random build names that don't sort well and mean nothing a week later. Two different builds with the same version string in-game. QA filing bugs against "latest_PC_build.zip" and nobody knowing which branch or date that was. Over-designed versioning schemes that look great in a doc but are too complicated for people to follow when they're tired and in a hurry. Simple, consistent labels and a visible version number beat "final_final3" every single time.

Topic: .... Date: ....

Minimal Documentation That's Enough

If nobody reads it or uses it to make decisions, it's not documentation – it's noise.
You don't need a perfect wiki to ship a game. You also can't run a serious project on "it's all in our heads and in chat history". The sweet spot is just enough, kept alive, tuned to the size of your team and game. What "enough" looks like will change from project to project – but one rule never changes: if it's important and not written anywhere, expect confusion later.

Three kinds of docs

Think less about formats, more about how long the document should matter.

1. Living docs – must stay current

These are the few documents that lose value fast if they're outdated. They need a clear owner.
Typical examples:

- Game vision one-pager – the current "why this game exists" in one page.
- High-level roadmap snapshot – what we're roughly doing over the next months.
- "How we work" basics – where the board is, when we meet, how we release, where decisions live.

If a living doc goes stale, it quietly creates diverging versions of reality in people's heads.

2. Reference docs – OK to age a bit

These capture how something works at a point in time. They're useful when you need depth, but nobody expects them to reflect every small change.
Examples: a deeper feature spec, a technical overview, a content style guide, notes from a spike. They're good to have when someone asks "why is it like this?" six months later.

3. Throwaway docs – use and forget

These exist to help you think or align right now: workshop notes, scratchpads, early exploration docs. Once they've done their job (decision made, direction chosen), they can be archived or deleted.
The trick is to make sure any real decisions they produced are captured in a living doc or a simple decision log, not only trapped in a screenshot of a whiteboard.

Most teams suffer not from "too few docs", but from not knowing which doc is which.

Ask three questions before writing anything

Before you create yet another document, ask:

1. Who is this for?

New hires? Current team? External partner? Future you in six months? If you can't answer, you probably don't need it.

2. When will they use it?

During onboarding, in planning, when debugging, when making a go/no-go call? If there's no clear moment of use, it will rot.

3. Who owns keeping it true enough?

Not "the team". A real person or role. If nobody owns it, it will drift and start hurting more than it helps.
If you don't have good answers to at least two of these, don't write the doc. Put that time into fixing a doc that already matters.

Try this

On the right page, take a honest look at your documentation.

1. List the documents your project currently has that people actually talk about: specs, roadmaps, notes, whatever. Don't overthink, just write what comes to mind.
2. Next to each, mark it as Living, Reference or Throwaway based on how you really use it, not how you wish you used it.
3. Now choose 3–5 documents you believe your project truly needs as core. For each one, note:
   - who it's for,
   - when they will use it,
   - who owns keeping it "true enough".

If some existing docs don't fit into any of those 3–5, it might be time to archive or ignore them on purpose instead of pretending they matter.

Watch out

Huge document dumps nobody reads, created because "we should have documentation". Specs that are beautiful on day one and poisonous six months later because they no longer match the game. Decisions made in calls and chats that never make it into anything searchable, so you re-fight the same battles over and over. Minimal documentation is not about doing the least possible. It's about writing only what the team will actually use, and then caring enough to keep those few things alive.

Topic: .... Date: ....

When to Escalate – To Whom, With What

If you escalate everything, people stop listening.
If you escalate nothing, you quietly sink the project.
As a producer or lead, part of your job is deciding which problems you solve locally and which you push up the chain. Escalation is not betrayal of your team. It's admitting, "This is bigger than my authority, my budget, or my reach – and if we don't change something above my level, this will keep hurting the project or the people."
The point is not to dump problems on someone else. The point is to get a decision or support you cannot get where you stand.

When it's time to escalate

Not every annoyance deserves an escalation. You're looking for patterns and impact. It's usually time to escalate when:

- A problem blocks the team repeatedly despite reasonable attempts to solve it locally.
- The impact crosses your boundaries: multiple teams, critical scope, key dates, important partners, people's health.
- The risk is bigger than your authority: budget, headcount, major scope cuts, cancelling or delaying external commitments.
- You see behaviour that is clearly harmful (burnout, toxic patterns, serious conflict) and you cannot fix it by talking to the people involved.

A single bad day is not an escalation. A repeated pattern that threatens delivery or people usually is.

To whom – and how high

Escalation should go to the lowest level that can actually change the situation.
If it's about priorities or day-to-day decisions inside your team, you probably escalate to a discipline lead, project owner or your direct manager. If it affects multiple projects, budget, company strategy or serious people issues, you go higher – but still with the same goal: reach someone who can say "we're doing X, not Y" and make it stick.
Escalation is not the same as venting sideways to someone powerful. You escalate to the person who owns the area where the root cause sits: production, tech, HR, business, publishing, leadership.

With what – structure your escalation

Whether you send a message, write a note or prepare for a live conversation, keep a simple structure in your head:

- Context – what this is about, in one or two clear sentences: the area, the team, the time frame.
- What's happening – concrete description of the pattern, not just "things are bad". What have you observed? How often? For how long?
- Impact – what this costs: missed milestones, wasted time, broken trust, risk to launch, risk to people. The more specific, the better.
- What you've tried – the local actions you already took: conversations, process tweaks, compromises, changes in your own behaviour. Show that escalation is not your first move.
- What you need – the decision, support or intervention you're asking for. For example: a clear priority, more or fewer people on something, a change in scope, backing for a process change, help with a conflict.

This works both in writing and in a spoken escalation. Often it's worth sending a short written summary even after a call, so nobody misremembers what was agreed.

Try this

On the right page, look at three recent situations from your project:

1. One where you did escalate. One where you should have escalated but didn't. One where you escalated too early or too loudly. For each, write a few lines: what happened, what you did, what the outcome was.
2. For each case, rewrite what a clean escalation would have looked like using the structure above: Context / What's happening / Impact / What we've tried / What we need.
3. From these reflections, sketch your own personal rules for this project:

When do I try to solve it locally only? When do I escalate with a calm message or note? When do I ask for a live conversation because the topic is too sensitive or complex for text?
Keep this page as a reference. The goal is not to escalate more or less. The goal is to escalate deliberately: rarely, clearly, and with enough information that the person above you can actually help instead of guessing.

Watch out

Escalating every irritation until people tune you out. Escalating nothing, then acting surprised when leadership discovers a disaster too late to react. Using escalation as a way to attack individuals instead of describing patterns and impact. And, on the flip side, trying to "handle everything yourself" long after it's obvious that the problem sits above your pay grade. Good escalation is a professional skill: clear, specific, focused on outcomes – and used when the project or the team genuinely needs more power than you have alone.

Topic: .... Date: ....

Production Anti-patterns – Behaviours That Break Projects

These patterns don't kill projects in one day – they slowly rot them from the inside.
Most teams don't decide to work badly. Anti-patterns appear as shortcuts, "temporary" hacks or coping mechanisms, then harden into normality. As a producer or lead, your job is not to pretend they don't exist. Your job is to see them early, name them clearly, and push back before they become the only way the project works.
This page is not a complete catalogue, just a set of examples you can recognise and adapt to your own reality.

Typical anti-patterns you should watch for

You'll see different flavours of the same behaviours across studios and projects:

- Permanent crunch / heroics – overtime becomes the default, and the same few people "save" every milestone. It looks productive in the short term, but burns trust, health and quality.
- Moving targets – goals, dates and priorities constantly shift without a clear reason or written decision. The team stops believing any plan and starts optimising for survival, not for the game.
- Secret decisions / shadow leadership – real decisions happen in private chats, side calls or a separate room in the office. The rest of the team just sees chaos and "mood swings" in direction.
- Fake deadlines – invented dates used to "motivate" people, then quietly moved. After a few rounds, nobody believes any deadline, including the real ones.
- No ownership / blurred responsibility – many people "kind of" own an area, so nobody really does. Problems bounce around because no one feels it's clearly their job to decide or fix.
- Endless "later", no cutting – everything is still "on the table". Nothing is truly dropped, only postponed. Scope quietly outgrows reality until cuts happen in panic, not by design.
- Meetings instead of decisions – issues are discussed over and over, but nothing is resolved. People leave calls with different understandings and no clear "who does what next".

These patterns are common in gamedev because there's always another build, another event, another dependency. That doesn't make them harmless.

Your role as producer or lead

You won't fix all of this alone, and some anti-patterns sit above your pay grade. But you do control how you run your area:

- You can insist that decisions you depend on are written somewhere visible.
- You can refuse to treat fake dates as real, and ask openly which dates actually matter.
- You can protect your team from permanent crunch by pushing for scope cuts or renegotiating commitments.
- You can make ownership explicit: "this person owns X until we decide otherwise".
- You can be the one who says, "We've talked about this enough; here is the decision and the next step."

You're not trying to create a perfect world but only trying to stop the worst behaviours from becoming invisible background noise.

Try this

On the right page, look honestly at your current project.
First, list a handful of situations from the last few months that felt "wrong" from a production point of view: messy pushes, broken promises, constant fire drills, people burning out, meetings that never ended in decisions. Next to each, note which anti-pattern it smells like. It's OK if more than one applies.
Then pick two patterns that hurt you the most right now. For each, write in a few lines:

- how it shows up specifically in your project (concrete examples, not theory),
- what you can realistically do about it in the next month, given your role,
- who you need to talk to or align with to make that change stick.

Keep it small and practical: one rule you'll start enforcing, one habit you'll drop, one conversation you'll have.
Come back to this page after a couple of sprints or a milestone and mark what actually changed and what stayed the same. That feedback is part of your own production learning loop.

Watch out

Treating anti-patterns as "just how gamedev works" and giving up on them. Turning this list into a weapon to attack specific people instead of behaviours and systems. Trying to fix every problem at once and burning out on meta-work. And the classic: seeing the patterns clearly, talking about them in private, but never taking even a small visible step to push back. Naming an anti-pattern is useful. Changing one concrete behaviour around it is what actually moves the project.

Topic: .... Date: ....

Block D
Game Design & UX

Topic: .... Date: ....

Core Loop – Definition & Visualisation

If you can't explain your core loop in one sentence, you don't really have it.
The core loop is the repeating pattern of play that carries most of your minutes in the game. It's what the player actually does again and again when the tutorial is gone, the trailers are forgotten and they're just... playing. Everything else – meta, story, cosmetics, systems – either supports this loop or distracts from it.

A useful way to think about it:
Player does X → gets Y → is motivated to do Z → comes back to X
For example, without naming any specific game:
"Explore new areas → collect resources → upgrade gear → unlock tougher areas → explore again."
"Serve customers → earn currency → upgrade equipment and recipes → attract more demanding customers → serve again."
"Win short matches → gain ranking and rewards → unlock new options → queue for another match."
The words you choose matter a lot. They reveal whether your loop is about expression, mastery, collection, survival, creativity, social pressure, or something else. If the loop you write down doesn't match the fantasy you promised in your pillars and USP, you've found a problem worth solving early.

Core loop, game pillars and USP
Your core loop is the place where your game pillars and USP either come alive or quietly die.
If one of your pillars is "meaningful player choices", but your loop is "grind small tasks to slowly fill bars", you have a mismatch. If your USP is about "co-op kitchen chaos" but your loop is mostly solo inventory management, same story.
A good sanity check:

- Read your pillars and USP once.
- Then write your core loop sentence.
- Ask yourself: Would a player who only sees this loop feel those pillars and that promise?

You don't need a perfect answer, but you do need an honest one.

One sentence before diagrams
It's tempting to jump straight into pretty diagrams. Resist that for a moment. If you can't express the loop in one clear sentence, a drawing will only hide confusion.
Keep the sentence:

- short enough to fit in one line,
- concrete enough that someone outside the team could imagine what they'd be doing,
- focused on player actions and reactions, not on internal system names.

When the sentence feels solid, you can map it into a simple circle or sequence. Put actions on one side, results on the other.

Mark where you expect fun to spike and where friction can appear. This doesn't have to be art. It just has to force you to think.

Try this
On the right page, sketch a few possible core loops for your current game.
Start by writing three to five one-sentence loops using the pattern "Player does X → gets Y → is motivated to do Z → back to X". Let yourself try a couple of different angles: more combat-focused, more builder-focused, more social, more strategic. You're not committing yet; you're exploring.
Next to each sentence, note briefly:

- which game pillar(s) it clearly supports,
- how it connects to your USP,
- where you believe the moment-to-moment "fun" sits and where the biggest friction will be.

If you feel brave, add a tiny circle diagram for the one or two variants that seem strongest: actions, rewards, motivation back into the loop. Don't over-polish; this is a thinking tool, not a pitch slide.

Once you have a few options, cross out the ones that clearly work against your pillars or USP, even if they sound cool in isolation. You're looking for something that fits the game you actually want to build, not just any nice loop.

Watch out
Core loops that are really just lists of systems, not what the player actually does. Loops that look impressive on paper because they have many steps, but in practice mean "press button, watch progress bar". Descriptions that hide boredom behind vague verbs like "engage", "interact", "experience" instead of naming what the player really does. And, most common in gamedev: falling in love with a loop that belongs to another game you admire, rather than to the pillars and USP you already defined for your own.

Topic: .... Date: ....

Meta Loop & Progression – Structure Above the Core Loop (1)

If your meta loop doesn't make the core loop more interesting, it's just padding.
The core loop is what the player does minute to minute. The meta loop is what gives those minutes long-term meaning: where progress lives, where collections grow, where the player feels the game "moving forward" over days and weeks, not just seconds.
A simple way to separate them:

- Core loop: "What am I doing right now?"
- Meta loop: "Why does doing this again still matter for me later?"

Upgrades, unlocks, collections, world changes, narrative arcs, rankings, base-building, long-term goals – that's all meta. It sits around the core loop and shapes why the player comes back.

Meta must support core loop, pillars and USP

The meta loop is not its own game stapled on top. It should amplify the fantasy you already committed to in your pillars, USP and core loop, not fight it.

If your pillars talk about creativity and expression, meta progression that only pushes raw power will feel off. If your USP is about tight, tense matches, meta that forces daily chores and long grinds for tiny stat boosts will undercut that promise.
A quick alignment test:

1. Read your pillars and USP once.
2. Read your core loop sentence from D50.
3. Ask: "If I extend this loop over weeks, what should feel bigger, deeper, richer for the player?"

Your meta loop should be a clear answer to that question. Yes, it can help retention. Yes, it can support monetisation if that's part of the business. But if the player fantasy disappears and only charts and currencies remain, you've gone too far.

Thinking in horizons of progression

Progression is easier to reason about if you think in time horizons, not in systems first. Start from what the player feels, then back into mechanics.
Roughly:

- Short horizon – minutes to first sessions. The player should quickly see something move: a bar filling, a level gained, a small unlock, a visible change. This is about "I'm not wasting my time".
- Medium horizon – a few sessions, a few evenings. The player starts to feel direction: a build coming together, parts of the world opening, a collection taking shape, a storyline advancing. This is where you support commitment.
- Long horizon – many sessions over weeks. The player sees identity and legacy: who they have become in the game, what they own or control, what they have achieved that a new player clearly hasn't.

For each horizon, the question is: "What changes for the player if they keep engaging with the core loop?" Not: "How many bars can I add?"

Once you know what should change, you can decide whether that means levels, unlock trees, collections, narrative beats, base upgrades, rankings, or something else.

Meta loop as a frame around play

A simple way to visualise it:

- In the centre: your core loop from D50 – the repeated play.
- Around it: one or more circles representing the meta tracks that grow when the player runs that loop.
- Above it all: a small note on what the player is ultimately trying to achieve in this game world.

If the outer circles don't clearly feed back into making the core loop more engaging, satisfying or meaningful, they're probably bloat. If they demand grind without changing the moment-to-moment experience, they're just chores wearing progression clothes.

Topic: .... Date: ....

Meta Loop & Progression – Structure Above the Core Loop (2)

Try this
On the right page, map the progression horizons for your current game.
Start by writing one sentence for each horizon: short, medium, long. Stay at the fantasy level, not systems. Focus on what the player feels changes in their experience if they keep playing.

Under each sentence, note which parts of your current design already support that feeling, and which are missing or pulling in a different direction. Then, next to your core loop from D50, sketch how running that loop feeds into each horizon: what the player gets now, what they see after a few sessions, what's different for them after many.

If you notice that most rewards live only in one horizon (for example everything is short-term, or everything is long grind), mark that clearly. That's a design decision – or a gap.

Watch out
Meta loops designed mainly for charts: daily checklists, fake urgency, grind for the sake of "retention", with little connection to what's actually fun to play. Progression systems that throw in more and more currencies and tracks until nobody on the team can explain them in plain language. Long-term goals that sound impressive, but don't meaningfully change the core play – the player just does the same thing with slightly bigger numbers. And the opposite: ignoring progression completely and hoping the core loop alone will carry players for dozens of hours, even when the fantasy clearly calls for growth, change and visible evolution over time.

Topic: .... Date: ....

Player Journey – First 30 Minutes

If you lose players in the first 30 minutes, you basically lose them for good.
Those first minutes are not about showing everything your game can do. They are about giving the player a clear direction, a reason to care, and the feeling that this world makes sense. Systems, lore and features all come later. Here, the questions are simple:

- Do I understand what I'm doing right now?
- Do I know what I'm trying to achieve next?
- Do I feel like this might be worth my time?

Think of the first 30 minutes from the inside of the player's head, not from your feature list.

What the first 30 minutes should do
Roughly, you can treat them in three phases:

- 0–5 minutes – Arrival and first control
- The player decides if they even want to try. They need a quick sense of the world, a first meaningful input, and a clear short-term goal. Confusion or long walls of text here cost you heavily.
- 5–15 minutes – First successes and first small problems
- The player should feel: "I can do things, the game reacts, I'm starting to get it." Here you set the tone of your core loop and show the first consequence of their choices. They need a direction more than they need depth.
- 15–30 minutes – Direction and potential
- Now they should be thinking: "I know what this game is about, and I see why it might get interesting later." They should have a visible medium-term goal, a sense of progression starting, and a hint of what the game can become if they stay.

At every step, ask: What does the player see? What do they think is going on? What do they feel pulled toward?

Journey, not feature checklist
It's easy to plan the first 30 minutes as: "We must show system A, mechanic B, UI area C." From the player's point of view, that's just noise if it doesn't build a coherent journey.
Instead, focus on beats:

- the moment they first take control;
- the first clear sign of "you did the right thing";
- the first time something goes wrong in a safe way;
- the moment they understand "this is what this game really is";
- the first visible step toward a bigger goal.

Direction matters more than completeness. The player doesn't need to know everything. They need to know enough to want the next step.

Try this
On the right page, map the first 30 minutes of your game as a journey, not as a design document.
Draw a simple horizontal line and split it into four segments: 0–5, 5–10, 10–20, 20–30. For each segment, write short notes answering four questions:

- What does the player see first when this segment starts?
- What do they understand they should be doing?
- What do they experience in terms of success, failure, or surprise?
- What clearly moves them forward toward a goal?

Then, underneath the line, mark three specific beats: the first moment of control, the first real success, and the first time the longer-term direction of the game becomes obvious. If you struggle to place these, that's already a useful signal.

Finally, in the margin, write one sentence:
"If a stranger stopped playing at minute 30, how would they describe what this game is about and what they were trying to achieve?"
If you don't like the answer, you know where to improve.

Watch out
Opening sequences that talk too much and let the player do almost nothing. First minutes where the player technically can move, but has no idea why or toward what. Throwing systems and UI elements at them with no sense of priority, then being surprised when they bounce off. And, very common, assuming that players will "push through the early confusion" to reach the good part later. In reality, the first 30 minutes are the game for a huge part of your audience. Treat that journey with the same care you give to any late-game feature.

Topic: .... Date: ....

Difficulty Curve – Basic Models

A bad difficulty curve doesn't feel "hard", it just feels unfair or boring.
Difficulty is not just numbers in a spreadsheet. It's the player's perceived journey from "I'm learning" through "I'm challenged" to "I'm good at this now". If the curve is off, players either check out because nothing demands effort, or quit because every step feels like a slap.

Think of difficulty as the shape of tension and mastery over time, not just enemy stats or level count.

Difficulty vs perceived difficulty
Raw difficulty is what the game throws at the player: speed, damage, complexity, number of things on screen.
Perceived difficulty is how it feels:

- do they understand what went wrong when they fail,
- do they see what they could try differently next time,
- do they feel the game is being fair, even when it's punishing.

Players will tolerate a lot of raw difficulty if they feel they're learning, getting better and being treated fairly. They won't tolerate moderate difficulty that feels random, unreadable or pointless.

Three simple curve archetypes
You don't need a perfect graph. You need a shape in your head.
A gentle ramp: difficulty slowly increases as the player learns. Early on there's more safety and forgiveness; later, less. This works well when you want broad accessibility and steady onboarding.
A wave with peaks: tension rises, then falls a bit, then rises higher. Think of arcs: build-up, intense section, release, next arc. This keeps players from burning out while still feeling like the game has teeth.
A spike then plateau: a high early hurdle, then a broad area where demand is steady but not constantly mounting. This can work when you want a clear "entry exam" that filters players, then a space for deep mastery at roughly the same level.
Most real games mix these ideas. What matters is that you choose a general model instead of accidentally drifting into "random chaos".

One curve rarely fits all
No single curve will be perfect for everyone. Different players arrive with different skills, patience and goals. You don't have to serve every possible person, but you should be honest about who you're designing for and give others basic tools.
Assist options, difficulty modes, aim aids, puzzle hints, extra time, optional challenges – all of these can let players shape their own curve a bit. The point is not to make the game trivial. It's to avoid forcing everyone through the exact same narrow tunnel.

If you find yourself constantly smoothing the curve for one group while making it harsher for another, you probably need more than one path.

Try this
On the right page, sketch your ideal difficulty curve in three acts.
Draw a simple line from left to right and split it into Act I, Act II, Act III. For each act, note in a few words how you want players to feel: how tense, how confident, how often they should fail, how often they should feel powerful. Mark roughly where you want the first real wall, the most intense peak, and the sections where players can breathe and feel strong.
Next to the line, write one sentence per act: "In this act, the player should feel…". Keep it about feelings and behaviour, not numbers. If you plan multiple modes or assists, quickly note how that shape changes for a less experienced and a more experienced player.

If the curve you draw is flat, full of random spikes, or climbs endlessly with no plateau for mastery, that's a signal to adjust before you build more content on top of it.

Watch out
Sudden difficulty spikes with no preparation or teaching, where players fail but don't know why. Long stretches with no real challenge, where players go into autopilot and then quit out of boredom. Designing a curve only for your best internal testers, then being shocked that regular players bounce off. And assuming "we'll adjust it later" without any clear idea of what "later" means or how you'll know the curve is actually doing its job.

Topic: .... Date: ....

Onboarding & Tutorial – Minimum Rules

If your tutorial feels like work, players will treat your game like work.
Onboarding is not there to show how much you have thought about the game. It is there to help a real human being arrive in an unknown world, understand what matters, and start doing interesting things as soon as possible. Everything else is optional.
The key tension is simple: the game must be understandable enough to play, but you must not choke the pace with explanations. Some games and audiences need more hand-holding, some can get away with almost none. The rule that does not change: teach just enough to let the player enjoy the next step, then get out of the way.

Teach in context, one thing at a time
Players remember what they do, not what they read. The safest pattern is:

1. put the player in a situation where a mechanic is useful or necessary,
2. show a clear, short hint of what to try,
3. let them do it with low risk,
4. reinforce success with feedback and a small reward.

You do not need to dump every control and system in the first room. You need to make sure that when a mechanic becomes relevant, the player has a fair chance of understanding it.
Even if your game is dense or aimed at experienced players, this rule holds. You can move faster, you can assume more knowledge, but you still teach in the moment where the mechanic matters, not in an abstract void.

Separate "must know" from "nice to know"
A lot of bad onboarding comes from treating every piece of information as equally urgent. It is not.
For the first minutes, ask yourself: what does the player absolutely need to know to act, survive and enjoy themselves? That is your "must know" set. Everything else can be discovered later, or offered as optional depth.
"Must know" usually covers basic movement and interaction, how to read health or failure, and one or two core verbs that define the game. "Nice to know" is advanced combos, edge-case rules, deep system explanations, lore details. If you try to push both at once, players will either ignore you or feel drowned.
Design your onboarding so that "must know" is taught clearly and early, and "nice to know" is offered when curious players go looking for it or when the situation really demands it.

Don't block the fun if you don't have to
The biggest sin of tutorials is blocking the actual game. Long unskippable sequences, forced steps that ignore what the player tries to do, scripted sections that treat them like a passenger.
Sometimes you genuinely need a short locked sequence to avoid overwhelming people or to prevent them from soft-locking themselves. Use this sparingly, and be honest with yourself: are you protecting the player, or just compensating for messy design with control?
Wherever possible:

- let the player move, look around and interact while learning;
- allow them to repeat instructions easily if they missed something;
- allow experienced players to skip or fast-forward early guidance without breaking the game.

There is no single correct style. A slow tactical game can afford a slower, more explicit onboarding. A fast action game needs to get to "doing the thing" very quickly. The point is to make the style match the tempo and fantasy of your game, not to apply a generic template.

Try this
On the right page, define what onboarding means for your current game.
First, write one sentence describing who your typical first-time player is and how fast the game itself wants to move. Then list, in plain language, the few things they must be able to do and understand after roughly ten minutes of play. For each item, note how you will teach it in a way that fits your pace: a quick prompt in the middle of action, a short guided moment in a safe space, a deliberate failure that explains itself, or a calm step-by-step interaction. Finally, mark anything you are currently explaining in those first minutes that is not truly needed yet. Decide whether to push it later, make it optional, or remove it entirely.

Watch out
Tutorials that read like manuals and ignore the actual flow of play. Forcing players through long, fully scripted sections "for their own good" when the real problem is unclear UI or overloaded controls. Treating onboarding as a separate mini-game that does not feel like the real experience. And assuming that once a tooltip has appeared once, the job is done. Onboarding is successful only when players forget it existed and simply feel that the game world makes sense under their fingers.

Topic: .... Date: ....

Feedback & Rewards – Information and Meaning

Games talk to players all the time. Most of that "conversation" is not text or VO – it's feedback and rewards. When this conversation is clear and aligned with your fantasy, players feel in control, powerful and curious. When it isn't, they feel lost, annoyed or numb.

A simple split:

- Feedback – what the game says immediately after an action.
- Rewards – what the game gives the player over time for engaging with the game.

Both should feel like they belong to this game, not to some generic "loot machine".

Moment-to-moment feedback

Feedback answers one core question: "What just happened and was it good or bad for me?"

It shows up in many channels at once: what the player sees, hears, feels and reads. Even if your game is calm or abstract, the player still needs to know when they did something right, wrong, risky or special.

Useful channels to think about:

- Visual – animations, flashes, highlights, screen shake, UI changes.
- Audio – hits, misses, UI beeps, stingers for special moments, silence when something fails.
- Haptics / feel – controller vibration, camera movement, timing changes, input response.
- System feedback – health, scores, meters, logs, messages, state changes in the world.

Good feedback is fast, readable and consistent. The player shouldn't have to guess whether they hit, missed, succeeded, failed, took damage or triggered something important.

If a player repeatedly asks "Why did this happen?" after basic actions, your feedback is too weak or too noisy.

Rewards: short, medium, long

Rewards answer a different question: "Why should I keep doing this?"

They should be tightly connected to your core loop, meta loop and fantasy. In practice, think in horizons:

- Short-term rewards – immediate or near-immediate: points, currency, drops, small story beats, quick visual celebrations. They confirm that the last few actions mattered.
- Medium-term rewards – things you reach after a session or a few: meaningful upgrades, new options, new areas, new tools, unlocks that change how you play. These build a sense of progress and direction.
- Long-term rewards – goals that shape identity and long commitment: big unlocks, endgame systems, collections, reputation, transformational story outcomes.

All three should feel like they belong to the same fantasy. If your game is about being a scrappy underdog, your rewards should not suddenly turn you into a generic superhero without the game world reacting. If the fantasy is craft and mastery, pure raw power rewards will feel off.

Rewards also anchor progression and meta. If your "rewards" don't change what the player can do or how the world responds, they are decoration, not progression.

Try this

On the right page, map how your game currently gives feedback and rewards.

First, pick your core loop sentence from D50 and write it at the top. Under it, list the key player actions inside that loop: attacks, builds, solves, sells, crafts, explores – whatever is central for your game.

For each action, note briefly:

- what feedback the player gets right now, in plain language;
- what they get as a short-term reward;
- what this action contributes to over the medium and long term.

Be honest: if an action has weak or confusing feedback, or rewards that don't really matter, mark it clearly. If you see actions that players do all the time but that barely connect to any meaningful reward, circle them. Those are usually the places where your game feels grindy or flat.

Watch out

Feedback that is so subtle players never notice it, or so loud that everything feels equally important. Rewards that look impressive on screen but don't change how the game plays or how the player feels. Systems that shower players with "stuff" until nothing has weight, and nobody remembers why they got what. And, more quietly, feedback and rewards that technically function but don't match the core fantasy you promised – leaving players with a game that works, but doesn't feel like the one they thought they were buying.

Topic: .... Date: ....

Economy Basics – Currencies, Sources & Sinks

If your economy doesn't support the game fantasy, it will feel like a job, not a world.
Game economy is just a structured answer to three questions:
What do players earn? Where from? What do they spend it on?
If those answers support your core loop and fantasy, the game feels coherent and rewarding. If they don't, you get grind, confusion and "why am I even doing this?".

Currencies: what matters in your world

A currency is anything the player can accumulate and later trade for something else. It doesn't have to be money. It can be resources, points, reputation, tickets, energy, crafting parts, trust with a faction.
The key is purpose. For each currency you introduce, you should be able to finish one simple sentence:
"This exists so the player can [do what?] in [which part of the game?]."
If you can't answer that clearly, the currency is probably noise. Too many currencies make the game feel like a bookkeeping exercise instead of a clear fantasy. Fewer, well-defined ones are almost always easier to balance and easier for players to understand.

Sources: how the world pays the player

Sources are where currencies come from: actions, systems, events, time. Ideally, they should connect directly to your core loop and to behaviours you actually want to encourage.
You choose what the world "pays for". If you reward only safe, repetitive actions, players will optimise for those and your game will feel like a chore. If you reward risk, mastery, exploration or creativity, players will lean into those.
When you define sources, ask yourself:

- Does this reward connect to what the game is really about?
- Does the player understand why they received it right now?
- Does this source help or hurt the fantasy?

If the answer to "why did I just get this?" is unclear, you're creating confusion instead of satisfaction.
Sinks: where value goes and why it feels good
Sinks are what the player spends currencies on: upgrades, unlocks, cosmetics, progress, shortcuts, repairs, entry fees, story beats.
Without real sinks, players quickly hit a state of "too rich to care". Numbers go up, but nothing in their experience changes. With badly designed sinks, you get the opposite: the world feels like it is constantly taxing them for breathing.
Good sinks:

- change what the player can do or how they express themselves,
- feel clearly connected to the effort they invested,
- make the game more interesting after the purchase, not less.

A sink is not a punishment. It's the moment where accumulated value turns into a new possibility.

Economy supporting fantasy and loop

Your economy should feel like a natural extension of your fantasy and core loop, not a separate mini-game layered on top.
If the fantasy is "running a small, struggling shop", the economy should reflect careful trade-offs and imperfect abundance, not endless fountains of cash. If the fantasy is "being an over-the-top hero", the economy can be more generous but still needs structure to avoid turning everything into meaningless excess.
Be careful when adding loops "for retention" or monetisation. If the economy stops serving the fantasy and starts serving only graphs, players will feel it, even if they can't explain why.

Try this

On the right page, sketch the basic economy of your current game in the simplest possible way.
First, list your main currencies by name. Next to each, jot down briefly where they primarily come from (sources) and what the player mainly uses them for (sinks). Finally, mark which currency is most tightly tied to your core loop – the one that really drives the main play – and which ones might be unnecessary or could be merged.
You're not designing formulas here. You're checking whether your economy has a clear, understandable skeleton that supports what the game is supposed to feel like.

Watch out

Adding new currencies every time you hit a design problem instead of fixing the underlying loop. Rewarding players heavily for behaviour that has nothing to do with the game's core fantasy. Economies with plenty of income but almost nothing worth spending on, or the opposite – constant drains with no sense of growth. And, quietly dangerous, relying on grind to stretch playtime when the underlying actions stopped being fun several hours ago. An economy that supports the fantasy and the core loop will usually need fewer moving parts than you think.

Topic: .... Date: ....

Level Design Quick-Notes – Flow, Readability, Pacing

If a player is lost, bored or annoyed, your level design has already failed – even if the layout is "clever".
You don't need a perfect theory of level design to improve things. You do need a small, honest set of questions you can ask every time you look at a level, no matter the genre. Think in three lenses: flow (how the player moves), readability (what they understand), and pacing (how tension rises and falls).

Flow – how the player actually moves
Flow is the path the player naturally takes, not the one you sketched in your first blockout.
Look at your level and ask:

- If I dropped a new player here with no explanation, where would they try to go first – and why?
- Are there obvious "current" lines in the space (paths, sightlines, affordances), or is everything equally flat?
- When the player moves from area to area, do transitions feel intentional (gate, landmark, change of scale), or like random corridors?

Good flow feels like the world is gently pushing the player forward, not like the designer is dragging them by the nose. You want enough guidance that players don't wander aimlessly, but enough freedom that they feel they're exploring, not riding a rail.

Readability – where to look, what matters
Readability is the difference between "challenging" and "confusing".
Ask yourself:

- Can a player tell, at a glance, which elements are interactive, dangerous, important, or just background?
- Is it obvious what is the next meaningful goal in this space (exit, item, objective, encounter), or do they have to pixel-hunt?
- Are you using contrast, lighting, colour, framing, motion or composition to guide attention – or is everything shouting at the same volume?

Players shouldn't need to fight the level to understand the basics. If people frequently miss doors, objectives or interactables that you consider critical, that's a readability issue, not a player issue.

Pacing – tension and breathing room
Pacing is the rhythm of pressure and relief. A flat line is almost always a problem.
Ask:

- Where in this level does tension clearly rise (more risk, more decisions, more enemies, more complexity)?
- Where does it clearly fall (safe area, vista, loot room, story beat, simple navigation)?
- If you plotted intensity over time, would you see any shape at all, or just a constant medium-level noise?

Good pacing alternates focus and release. Not every game needs dramatic peaks and valleys, but almost all benefit from moments where the player can reset, appreciate their progress and prepare mentally for the next push.

There are exceptions: some experiences deliberately overwhelm or disorient. That's fine – if it's a conscious choice that serves the game, not an accident.

Try this
On the right page, build a small, reusable checklist for your levels.
At the top, write three headings: Flow, Readability, Pacing. Under each, note 3–5 questions you want to ask yourself and your team for any new level or area, based on the prompts above. Keep the questions short and concrete, in your own words.
Then, think about the type of game you're making. Add one or two custom questions per section that fit your project's reality: for example, co-op visibility, stealth lines of sight, platforming clarity, narrative beats. The goal is not to capture every rule of level design – it's to have a focused set of sanity-check questions that actually get used.

You can revisit this page after a few milestones and adjust the checklist as you learn what really goes wrong in your project.

Watch out
Levels where players don't know where to go next and end up circling the same space without learning anything. Spaces where everything has the same visual weight, so objectives and exits are hidden in plain sight. Long stretches of identical pressure with no variation, where players slowly disconnect even if they technically "progress". And on the other side, remember: there are always exceptions. Some games want players to be lost for a while, or to feel relentless pressure. The point is to break your own rules on purpose, not because you never had any.

Topic: .... Date: ....

UX Heuristics for Games – Practical List

If the player is never sure what the game wants from them, that's a UX failure, not a skill issue.
You don't need a big UX book in your head. You need a small set of rules you can check your game against. These heuristics are not laws – they're practical lenses. Break them only on purpose.

Core heuristics for game UX

1. Always show: where I am, what I can do, what's active
At any moment, a player should be able to tell what state they're in (combat, menu, dialogue), what inputs make sense right now, and which systems are currently affecting them.
2. Don't punish learning
Early mistakes should teach, not humiliate. When a player tries something reasonable and it fails, the game should explain why and offer a clear next attempt, not quietly take away resources and say nothing.
3. One input, one meaning – per context
Within a given context, a button should do one clear thing. If you must reuse inputs, keep the context shift obvious (different mode, different camera, different UI) and avoid changing meanings without strong feedback.
4. Important information lives where the player looks
Critical info (health, countdowns, objectives, alerts) should be near the centre of attention, not hidden in a corner. Players look at the character, the crosshair, the immediate environment – put key signals in those sightlines.
5. The game explains state changes, not just states
It's not enough to show that something is active or on cooldown. The player should understand when and why it changed: I took damage, I triggered a power, I got debuffed, I gained a buff.
6. HUD serves the moment, not the feature list
The screen shouldn't show everything at all times. Default to what's needed for the current activity. Extra panels, logs, stats and meters can exist, but they should be collapsible, secondary or tied to specific modes. Some dense sims are exceptions – but even they benefit from a clear hierarchy.
7. Objectives in plain language
The game's current ask should be readable and concrete: "Reach the tower and activate the switch" beats "Progress the mission". If multiple objectives exist, make clear which is main, which is optional.
8. Actions feel like they land
When the player does something that matters – hits, blocks, crafts, confirms a choice – the game should respond with clear visual, audio and systemic feedback. If an action is important but feels soft, players will assume it doesn't work or isn't worth using.

These are starting points. Your specific game will add its own rules, but ignoring these almost always hurts.

Try this
On the right page, run a quick heuristic pass on your current game.
First, read the list above and mark two or three heuristics you believe are strong points of your project right now. Under each, note one concrete situation in the game where this strength is visible.
Then mark two or three heuristics you suspect you're breaking the most. For each, write a short example from the current build: where players get confused, mis-press, miss information or feel blind. Avoid theory; stick to real screens and moments.
Finally, choose one of the weak heuristics and note one small change you could try in the next iteration – a clearer prompt, a reduced HUD element, a better state change effect, a simplified input mapping. The goal is to use the list as a tool for action, not just for critique.

Watch out
Hidden systems with almost no feedback, where players are clearly affected but never told how or why. Changing the meaning of the same button across similar situations with no obvious context shift. HUDs that grow one icon at a time until nobody on the team can explain what half of them are for. And on the other side, stripping away so much information in the name of "minimalism" that players lose track of their state completely. These heuristics won't design the game for you, but they will catch many of the patterns that quietly make otherwise good mechanics feel unfair, noisy or opaque.

Topic: .... Date: ....

Accessibility Basics – Small Things, Big Impact (1)

You won't fix everything for everyone, but doing nothing is a choice too.
Accessibility is not an all-or-nothing certification. It's a set of concrete decisions that make your game easier to see, hear, control and process for real people with real constraints. Many of those decisions are small, cheap and entirely within reach of most teams – as long as you think about them before the very end.
The goal here is simple: make your game less tiring and more playable for more players, without turning production upside down.

A practical mindset

Accessibility is not a separate feature; it's a quality of everything you build.
You don't have to solve every possible case. You do need to ask: "Who am I excluding by default, and what low-cost changes could reduce that?" If you can, you later bring in experts or playtesting with people who have specific needs. But even before that, you can raise the baseline a lot with common sense.
Also: don't park everything under "post-release patch if we have time". Most of those patches never happen.

Key areas you can influence

Think in a few simple categories and do something in each.

Text and UI readability

Players need to read your UI and subtitles without squinting. That usually means font sizes that work on a sofa and at a desk, clear spacing, and avoiding ultra-thin decorative fonts for anything important. If you have a lot of text, consider at least one larger-size option or a "text scale" setting.

Colours and contrast

Relying only on colour to signal state (good/bad, active/inactive, friend/foe) will lock some people out. Simple fixes: distinct shapes or icons in addition to colour, clear contrast between text and background, and an option that reduces very bright flashes or heavy post-process effects. You don't need a perfect colourblind mode to make life much easier.

Controls and input flexibility

Different players have different hands, devices and abilities. Remappable keys and buttons, sensitivity options, hold vs toggle choices for key actions – these are not luxury features. Even partial flexibility (e.g., remapping primary actions) is better than a fixed, opaque layout. Make it clear what input is bound to what, and avoid complex chord inputs for basic actions.

Audio and noise

Not everyone plays with perfect hearing or any sound at all. Subtitles with speaker indication, visual cues for critical audio-only events, and separate sliders for effects, music and voice help a lot. Reducing constant background noise and giving players control over volume layers can turn an exhausting game into a manageable one.

Tempo and cognitive load

Some players need more time to read, react or process. Text that auto-advances too fast, QTEs that require very tight windows, or menus that close themselves while the player is still thinking can all be barriers. Where it fits your game, consider options that slow certain timings down, or at least avoid tying critical information to very short-lived messages.
There are many more areas – motion sickness, camera shake, pattern sensitivity – but starting with these already moves the needle.

Where experts and playtests fit

If you have the budget and time, bringing in someone who specialises in game accessibility or running playtests with players who have specific needs will always give you better insight than guessing. But that does not replace doing the basics; it builds on them. Expert help is most effective when you already treated accessibility as part of design, not as a last-minute checklist.

Topic: ....   Date: ....

Accessibility Basics – Small Things, Big Impact (2)

Try this

On the right page, take a clear look at your current project.

First, quickly rate yourself in the five areas above: text/UI, colours/contrast, controls, audio, tempo. For each, write one sentence: "Right now, our game is..." – be honest, not diplomatic.

Then, based on that snapshot, choose three small, realistic changes you could implement before the project ships that would help more players actually play and enjoy the game. Write what each change is, which area it touches, and who in the team would need to be involved.

If you already know someone in your network who cares deeply about accessibility, note their name and how you might sanity-check your ideas with them later. You're not committing to a full audit; you're building a habit of asking the question.

Watch out

Telling yourself "our game is too small for accessibility" while spending more time on purely cosmetic features. Leaving all accessibility decisions until content lock and then claiming it's impossible to change anything. Adding an "accessibility" menu that is just a couple of checkboxes nobody tested. And quietly assuming that because you personally can play comfortably, most players will be fine. You won't cover every need, but each thoughtful option you add makes it more likely that someone who would otherwise bounce off your game can stay and actually experience what you built.

Topic: .... Date: ....

Telemetry in Practice – Minimal Events

If telemetry doesn't lead to decisions, it's just an expensive hobby.
Telemetry is there to help you see what players actually do, not to produce pretty dashboards. For most teams, the problem is not a lack of data – it's logging the wrong things, logging too much, or never turning numbers into action.
A simple rule: start with questions, then design events. Not the other way around.

Telemetry serves questions, not tools
Before you add a single event, write down what you want to learn. Examples:

- Do players finish the tutorial, and where do they drop out?
- How long is a typical first session?
- Which systems are almost never touched?
- Where do players die or fail most often?

Only when you have questions like these does it make sense to ask: "What minimal set of events would give us answers?" Without clear questions, you will drown in logs that nobody uses.

Also: decide who will look at the data and when. If no one has time or responsibility for it, don't pretend telemetry will magically improve the game.

A minimal starter set (adapt, don't copy)
Every game is different, but if you log nothing else, consider a very small backbone like this:

- Session start / end – when players begin and stop playing, so you can see session lengths and basic retention.
- Tutorial start / completion / exit point – to see how many people you lose before they even reach the game.
- Key progression milestones – first core loop completion, first upgrade, first major unlock.
- Critical failure points – repeated deaths or abandons in specific levels, missions or encounters.
- Use of major systems – whether players ever touch crafting, co-op, advanced mechanics, or other key features.

This is not a complete recipe. It's a nudge: think in terms of a backbone, then add or remove events based on the questions your project actually cares about.

If an event doesn't help answer a real question or support a real decision, strongly consider not logging it.

IDs and consistency matter
Even a minimal setup is useless if you can't reliably connect the dots.
Whatever you log, keep naming and structure consistent: the same event name for the same action, stable identifiers for levels, missions, systems. Avoid renaming things every other build. Future you – or a specialist you bring in later – will thank you.

Clean, consistent telemetry is much easier for an external analyst to plug into. Messy, ad-hoc logs will cost you extra time and money before anyone can say anything meaningful.

Try this
On the right page, design a first-pass telemetry skeleton for your game.
Start by writing down three questions you'd genuinely like to answer after release. For each question, note:

- what part of the game it touches (onboarding, mid-game, endgame, a specific system),
- who in the team would use the answer (producer, designer, UX, marketing, leadership),
- what type of decision it might influence (scope changes, balancing, tutorials, feature priority).

Then, under each question, list the one to three events you would need to log to move from "guessing" to "knowing enough to act". Keep the event descriptions simple and tied to player actions or clear game states; don't worry about exact parameter lists here.

Finally, circle the events that appear in more than one answer. Those are your core telemetry candidates – the ones most likely to be worth the implementation and maintenance cost.

Watch out
Logging everything you can think of "just in case", then never looking at it. Designing events around engine internals instead of player behaviour, so nobody outside the code team can read them. Shipping a game with a huge analytics setup but no one clearly responsible for reviewing the data and proposing changes. And, just as bad, rejecting telemetry entirely because "we're a creative team" – then spending months arguing about things real players could have told you in a week. Telemetry doesn't replace design judgement, but a small, well-thought-out set of events can make that judgement a lot less blind.

Topic: .... Date: ....

Balancing Workflow – Iterations & Sanity Checks

If your balancing workflow is "change numbers until nobody complains", you don't have a workflow.
Balancing is not magic or taste-only. It's a repeatable loop: you decide what you want the player to feel, you set numbers and rules, you test, you look at feedback and data, and then you change things with intent. The goal of this page is simple: make that loop explicit and give you a few sanity checks that stop balance from drifting into chaos.

Balancing as a loop, not a one-off

Think of a basic cycle:

1. Assumption – "We want early weapons to feel safe but not boring; stronger ones should be exciting but come with trade-offs."
2. Implementation – you pick damage, health, cooldowns, costs, drop rates, etc.
3. Testing – internal play, focused playtests, maybe some early external players.
4. Signals – what people say (qualitative), what you observe, and what telemetry tells you.
5. Adjustment – you change numbers, rules, or content based on those signals.
6. Note why – one line: "Buffed shotgun damage because nobody used it in early game."

If you skip step 1 (assumption) and step 6 (note why), you still spin the loop – but nobody remembers what "good" was supposed to look like, or why numbers ended up where they are.

Sanity checks for any system

Whatever you're balancing – weapons, enemies, economy, missions – there are a few questions that always help:

- Is there a real choice? If one option is clearly dominant, players who optimise will all converge on it, and others will feel punished for not doing so.
- Is the risk–reward ratio clear? Higher risk must come with visibly higher reward, not just theoretical value.
- Is the early experience fair? The first hour should teach, not humiliate. If you want a punishing game, ramp into it.
- Does power growth feel earned? If upgrades barely change behaviour, they're fake progress. If they explode power too fast, the rest of the game collapses.
- Does this match your pillars? A "tactical" game where spam wins is out of tune with itself.

You don't need a spreadsheet for all of this. You do need to ask these questions regularly and answer them honestly.

Where your signals come from

Good balancing mixes feel, sessions, and numbers.

- Your own play and team play tell you how a system feels at a high level: is it frustrating, boring, spiky, trivial?
- Structured playtests with people closer to your target audience show how real players behave when they don't know your intentions.
- Telemetry (even minimal, like in D60) shows what actually happens at scale: which options are picked, where players drop, where they farm, where they quit.

None of these signals is enough alone. Feel without data can lie. Data without play can miss context. The workflow is about connecting them and then changing things with a clear reason.

Try this

On the right page, pick one concrete system in your current game: for example, a weapon set, an upgrade tree, enemy waves, or your main currency.

1. At the top, write in one or two sentences what you want this system to do for the player (fantasy, role in the game, rough difficulty or power curve).
2. Under that, describe your current balancing loop in 4–6 short lines:
   - how you pick starting values,
   - how often you revisit them,
   - what feedback or data you actually look at,
   - who has the final say.
3. Mark the weakest spot in that loop: no clear goal, no testing, no telemetry, no owner, no notes.
4. Finally, write down one change you could make in the next iteration to strengthen that weak spot – something small and realistic you can actually do.

Don't design a perfect future process. Capture how it really works today, and upgrade it by one step.

Watch out

Constantly "fixing" balance on a gut feeling after a couple of loud complaints, without testing or checking data. Balancing only for the strongest players on the team and then being surprised that regular players bounce off early. And letting numbers drift for months with zero written record of why they were changed, until nobody can tell if the system is "broken" or exactly as someone once wanted it.

Topic: .... Date: ....

Playtest Scenario Template – How to Plan a Session

"Just play and tell us what you think" is not a playtest. It's a random chat.

A good playtest session is designed on purpose. You know why you're running it, who you're inviting, what you're asking them to do, and how you'll use what you learn. This doesn't require a giant research team. It requires a simple, honest template you actually fill in before pressing "start".

Think of every session as a small experiment: you ask a few questions, you create conditions to answer them, you observe without steering, and you leave with something specific to change or confirm.

Scenario template

Use this structure as your one-page scenario skeleton.

1. Session goal – what are we trying to learn?

Write 2–3 clear questions. For example: "Do players understand their objective in the first area?" "Do they notice and use the crafting system?" Avoid vague goals like "see what they think of the game".

2. Player profile – who should play this?

Describe the type of player you want for this session: experience with the genre, familiarity with your project (first-time vs returning), platform they'll use. This keeps you from mixing very different profiles in one test and drawing messy conclusions.

3. Build & conditions – what exactly are we testing?

Note which build you're using, what content is unlocked, and any special constraints (debug tools disabled, god mode off, dev cheats hidden). The idea is to make sure everyone on the team remembers what the test actually looked like.

4. Tasks for the player – what will they try to do?

List a small set of tasks in natural language: "Reach the second area," "Complete one full core loop," "Craft one item," "Play one match." These are anchors, not a script. You want to see how they try to achieve them, not force a path.

5. What to observe – where do we look closely?

For each task or question, write what you'll pay attention to: where they hesitate, where they ask "what now?", what they fail repeatedly, what they ignore. Moderator and observers should know what moments are critical.

6. How we capture feedback – notes, questions, follow-up

Decide ahead of time: will you take live notes, record video, use a short survey, or run a debrief interview? Prepare 3–5 neutral questions for after the session ("What was the clearest part?", "What confused you?", "Where would you have stopped playing at home?"). Avoid leading questions like "Did you like X?" or "Wasn't Y annoying?"

Try this

On the right page, use your last messy playtest as a warm-up.

First, briefly describe a recent session that felt chaotic or unhelpful. Note what went wrong: goal too vague, tasks unclear, moderator talking too much, no notes taken, no decisions afterwards.

Then, using the template above, sketch a new scenario for the next playtest of a similar part of the game. Write your 2–3 main questions, define a rough player profile, list a few tasks, and decide how you'll observe and capture feedback. You don't need a perfect plan – just something concrete enough that another person on the team could run the session from this page.

Watch out

Trying to "test everything at once" in a single session and coming back with a bag of disconnected comments. Asking leading questions or explaining mechanics the moment a player struggles, instead of watching what they actually do. Letting the session end with no written notes, no clear answers to your original questions, and no follow-up actions. A playtest without a scenario is mostly therapy for the team. A simple, written plan turns it into a tool you can rely on across the whole project.

Topic: ....

Date: ....

Feature Evaluation – Goals → Observations → Decisions

If you don't make a decision after evaluating a feature, you've just wasted everyone's time.
Playtests, internal reviews, feedback rounds – they only matter if they end with a clear "keep / change / cut / postpone" and a rough idea of how. This page is a simple format you can use after any test of a feature or change, from a big new system to a small tutorial tweak.
Think of it as closing the loop: you define what success looks like, you observe what actually happened, and then you decide what you're going to do next – not "one day", but in this project, with this team.

Goals → Observations → Decisions

Use this structure as your default evaluation skeleton.

1. Goals for this feature / change

One short block that answers: "Why does this exist?"
Write 2–3 sentences in plain language:

- what this feature is supposed to do for the player (fantasy, experience, problem solved),
- how it's supposed to help the game (core loop, USP, progression, retention, business).

If you can't write this without hand-waving, you're not evaluating yet – you're still guessing what the feature is for.

2. What we observed / heard

This is where you collect signals, not opinions about opinions.
Capture:

- what players actually did (used it, ignored it, got stuck, abused it);
- what they said or asked unprompted;
- what internal testers noticed;
- any data you have (usage, win rate, completion rate, drop-offs).

Keep it factual: "Three out of five players never opened the map," "Most people used the new ability once and forgot it," "Telemetry shows only 10% of sessions reach this system."

3. What we conclude

This is the bridge between observations and action.
Summarise in a few lines:

- whether the feature currently meets its goals,
- what seems to be the main issue if it doesn't (visibility, clarity, balance, UX, timing in the journey).

You're allowed to say "we're not sure yet" – but only if you also say what you need to learn next.

4. What we will change

This is the decision part. Pick one of:

- Keep as is for now – and state why (it meets goals; other problems are more important).
- Iterate – what you will change and in which direction (stronger, simpler, clearer, earlier, later).
- Cut / shelve – remove it or park it, and note under what conditions it might return, if any.

Add "who owns this" and "by when do we expect the next check". It doesn't have to be a big deadline – just enough that it doesn't vanish into nothing.

Try this

On the right page, take the last feature or change you tested – big or small – and recreate the evaluation as if you had used this template.
First, write what the goal actually was. If you struggle, that's useful information.
Then, from memory and any notes you have, list the key observations: what people did, said, and what (if any) data you saw. Be honest about gaps: if you're guessing, mark it.
Next, write what you should have concluded at that time, and what decision should have been made – even if, in reality, you didn't formalise it or just "moved on".

Finally, underline whatever was missing: unclear goals, weak observations, or no explicit decision. That's your hint for what to do differently in your next feature evaluation.

Watch out

Endless rounds of "let's gather more feedback" without ever changing the feature or killing it. Mixing ten different goals into one evaluation ("it's for UX, and marketing, and balance, and monetisation") so nobody can say if it's working. Letting feedback pile up in documents that nobody reads, while the feature quietly calcifies in the build. A simple, written chain – goals → observations → decisions – doesn't make tough calls easier, but it makes sure they actually happen.

Topic: .... Date: ....

Kill Your Darlings – When to Remove "Cool" Things

Sometimes the most "fun" feature in the team's eyes is exactly what's dragging the project down.
"Kill your darlings" doesn't mean "cut everything that's interesting". It means being ruthless about keeping only what actually serves the game, players and project – even if you personally love the thing, even if a lot of work went into it.
You're not just protecting scope. You're protecting clarity.

Not everything that's good is good for this game
A feature can be: clever from a design point of view, technically impressive, fun in a vacuum,
...and still be a bad choice for the game.

A simple triad to check:

1. Alignment – Does it support the game's fantasy, pillars, core loop and USP, or pull attention sideways?
2. Player reality – Do real players use it, understand it and miss it when it's gone, or mostly ignore it?
3. Cost over time – How much does it cost to maintain, debug, explain, balance and carry this feature through to release and beyond?

If a darling scores weak on alignment and player reality, but very high on cost, you already know what the rational answer is. The hard part is accepting it.

A simple value vs cost check
When you're honest about it, many "nice" features land in one of four boxes:

- High value / low cost – obvious keep. These are the things that make your game what it is.
- High value / high cost – strategic decision. Maybe you keep it, but then other things must go to make room.
- Low value / low cost – candidates to simplify, merge or cut quietly. Often UI sugar, extra modes, one-off edge cases.
- Low value / high cost – the classic darling. Impressive in meetings, rarely used by players, always a pain for production.

You don't need a fancy matrix. You need to admit in which box a feature really sits, based on what you now know – not what you hoped at the start.

Who cuts, who advises
Someone has to own the knife. Usually that's the game director (or equivalent vision owner). They are the one who ultimately says: "This stays, this changes, this goes."
But good cuts are made with input, not in a vacuum. Designers, producers, programmers, art, QA – everyone can point at darlings that create pain: bugs that never die, systems nobody understands, tutorial parts that confuse every new player, content nobody reaches.

The director's job is to listen, weigh alignment, player reality and cost, and then make a clear call early enough that the team can adapt. The producer's job is to make sure this actually happens, instead of everyone quietly hoping that scope will magically fit.

Try this
On the right page, pick one feature or "cool idea" from your past projects that should probably have been cut earlier – even if it eventually shipped.
In a few lines, write:

- what it was supposed to do for the game and for players,
- how much work it actually took to build and maintain,
- what you saw in playtests or live usage (did people use it, understand it, care if it broke?).

Then, with the benefit of hindsight, answer honestly:

- Would the game have been significantly worse without it?
- What could that time and energy have been spent on instead?
- At what moment in the project did you have enough information to know it was a darling – and why wasn't it cut then?

Finally, write one sentence for your current project starting with:
"If I see a similar pattern again, I'll...".
That's your personal rule for the next time a "great idea" starts to quietly eat the schedule.

Watch out
Holding on to features just because a lot of work has already gone into them – the sunk cost trap. Keeping things only because they were "your" idea, so cutting them feels like losing an argument, not improving the game. Postponing hard decisions until very late, when cutting means breaking half the build instead of freeing up focus. And quietly avoiding the conversation, hoping that somehow everything will fit, even when everyone can see that it won't. Killing darlings hurts in the short term, but carrying them all the way to release usually hurts much more.

Topic: .... Date: ....

Block E
Business, Store & Marketing

Topic: .... Date: ....

Platforms & Business Models – Quick Map (1)

Platforms and business models are not a branding question. They decide who can even see your game, how money flows, what kind of production schedule you're committing to, and how long you'll be supporting the project after launch.
You don't need a perfect GDD for business on day one. You do need a rough map so the team isn't secretly building five different projects in their heads.

Two simple axes: where and how

For most projects you can think in two dimensions:

- Where the game lives – PC, console, mobile, handheld, cloud, sometimes VR.
- How value is captured – classic premium, premium + DLC/expansions, "complete edition" bundles, seasonal content, F2P, subscription / deal-based revenue.

A few common combos:
PC or console with a premium price and optional DLC is still the baseline for many projects: full experience at launch, expansions and content drops later. Players expect a solid core package and a clear value proposition.
Mobile skewing F2P or heavily discounted premium means reach can be huge, but it assumes you can handle retention, analytics, updates, and at least some user acquisition or featuring strategy. The business model is inseparable from live-ops.
Any platform with subscription deals or bundles (Game Pass-style, platform promos, third-party bundles) can help with exposure and guaranteed revenue, but you trade some control over price and discount timing for that stability.

There is no global "best" setup. The only useful question is: which combination fits this game, this team, this audience and this time window.

Sanity checks before you fall in love

Before the team gets emotionally attached to a dream platform or a trendy model, run a quick reality pass.
1. Does the model reinforce or fight your fantasy and core loop?
If the heart of the experience is a finite story, a forced grindy progression or aggressive monetisation will feel wrong to players and stressful to the team. If you're building an endlessly replayable sandbox, a one-off "fire and forget" premium sale might undersell its potential and mislead people about the long-term plan.
2. Can you actually deliver what the model silently demands?
Premium with a couple of DLCs still assumes patching, some content support and basic communication. F2P and live service assume a cadence of updates, balancing, events and operations. Multi-platform launches assume QA, certification and platform-specific work for each SKU. If you don't have budget or people for that, the model is not "ambitious", it's misaligned.
3. Where is your natural audience already playing?
Look at comparable games. Are they mostly on PC? Consoles? Mobile? Are they thriving on one main platform, or spread thin everywhere? If your fantasy and mechanics scream "controller on a couch", planning as if you were a PC-only title forever may not be honest. If your audience lives in niche PC genres, chasing mobile because "bigger market" can be a distraction.

If you cannot answer these questions without hand-waving, mark that uncertainty explicitly instead of pretending it doesn't exist.

One main path, everything else as phase two

It's fine to keep a long-term wish list: ports, extra platforms, different offers, maybe a service layer. The risk is trying to design for all of them at once: "PC now, maybe mobile later, maybe F2P hooks in case we pivot, maybe subscription if someone calls".
For the purposes of this notebook, assume you have to choose:

- One primary platform you design, test and market around.
- One primary business model you optimise the experience and content plan for.

Everything else lives in a "future options" box: good to keep in mind for UI, performance, and technical choices, but not allowed to distort every design discussion today. This kind of focus makes scope conversations, production planning and marketing alignment much easier later.

Topic: .... Date: ....

Platforms & Business Models – Quick Map (2)

Try this

On the right-hand page, sketch a simple two-axis map: platforms on one side, business models on the other.

Place a clear mark on the one combination that feels most realistic for your current project right now (for example "PC / Steam – premium with 1–2 DLCs").

Underneath, in a few short lines each, write:

- Why this combo supports your fantasy and core loop instead of fighting it.
- What kind of post-launch work this model implicitly requires from your team.
- Where players who like games similar to yours are actually spending time today.

Then add a second mark for a "phase two" option (for example "console port later" or "bundle/subscription deals if offered") and clearly label it as such. If you notice that most of your reasoning is "we'll decide later", highlight that – it's a signal to get clearer before production hardens around assumptions.

Watch out

Jumping into the newest shiny model because you've seen it in someone else's announcement. Designing like a giant live-service studio when you barely have enough people to ship a stable premium game. And promising every platform and every revenue stream at once, when you haven't yet made a single explicit decision about where players will discover your game and how they will pay for it.

Topic: .... Date: ....

Target Store Pages – Where Your Game Lives (1)

Your game does not "live on the internet". It lives in very concrete places: your Steam page, your PlayStation or Xbox store tile, a Nintendo eShop listing, a mobile store page, maybe a landing page somewhere. Each of these places has its own rules, templates and expectations.

If you pretend there is just one generic "store page", you'll either overbuild for a single platform or under-prepare for every platform at once.

One game, several front doors

For many teams, Steam is the first real front door: lowest friction to get in, huge discoverability challenges, but relatively flexible in terms of submission and iteration. When you are "only on Steam", store management is already a full-time concern around launch, but at least you are dealing with one set of inputs: one description, one tags system, one achievement set, one capsule family, one build channel.

The moment you go multi-platform (PlayStation Store, Xbox Store, Nintendo eShop, Epic, GOG, App Store, Google Play and so on), you are no longer running "one store page with different logos". You are maintaining multiple product entries, each with different asset requirements, regional constraints, text limits, platform features and certification processes. Even if the core pitch stays the same, the details do not.

The key decision here is not "do we want more players?" but "do we have the capacity to properly support more than one front door at the same time?"

Different platforms, different checklists

Every platform will ask you for some combination of: text (short and long descriptions, feature lists, age rating summaries), visuals (key art, capsules, banners, icons, screenshots, sometimes platform-specific promo assets), video (trailers, short clips, feature-specific videos), builds (binaries, branches, test builds, certification submissions), and compliance info (age ratings like PEGI/ESRB/USK, privacy and data use declarations, legal texts).

The catch: formats and rules are not identical, and they change over time. Image sizes get updated, new promo slots appear, guidelines for tags and features evolve, rating questionnaires are revised. Treating "requirements" as a checklist you copy once from a blog post is risky. For each platform you select, someone on the team should own the simple discipline of checking the current documentation before a big milestone and updating your internal notes.

What looks like a minor difference on paper ("banner ratio is slightly different here") turns into real work when multiplied by languages, regions and multiple concurrent versions of the game.

Steam-first vs multi-platform reality check

Using Steam as your primary reference is practical. It lets you prototype your pitch, visuals and wording in a relatively open environment, and you can use that as a baseline for other platforms later. But be honest about your trajectory.

If the plan is "Steam only for the foreseeable future", you can invest more deeply into optimising that single page and its update cycles. If the real ambition is "Steam now, consoles within a year", then it's worth sketching what those future store entries will demand from you: controller-first messaging, different hero art, stricter certification timelines, enforced regional pricing rules, additional rating processes.

The worst situation is telling yourself "we'll be everywhere" while nobody budgets time for extra asset sets, extra QA, and the admin overhead of multiple backends. Multi-platform is not just more revenue opportunities; it is more calendars and more moving parts.

Mapping your store ecosystem

For the purposes of this notebook, treat "target store pages" as a small ecosystem around your game, not a single item on a to-do list.

Think in terms of: which stores are realistic for us, what each one expects from us, and who is responsible for keeping that page coherent and up to date. Even if you end up choosing just one platform, the exercise of writing down what you would need for others will expose blind spots: missing age ratings, no plan for localisation of store text, no owner for screenshots, no process to keep descriptions aligned with the current build.

The earlier you draw this map, the fewer unpleasant surprises you get when a console partner asks for assets you never prepared, or a mobile submission gets delayed because you assumed last year's guideline still applies.

Topic: .... Date: ....

Target Store Pages – Where Your Game Lives (2)

Try this

On the right-hand page, list the 2–3 stores that are realistic targets for your current project (for example: Steam, one console store, one mobile store - or just Steam if that's the truth).

Under each store name, leave space and write a short line for:

- What text elements we need there (descriptions, feature blurbs, age rating statements).
- What visual and video assets we need (art, capsules/banners, screenshots, trailers).
- What builds and approvals we must go through (binaries, ratings, certification, technical checks).

Mark clearly which of these items you already have in at least "good enough" shape, and which are currently just wishful thinking. If a store is on the list but you cannot list its basic requirements without guessing, highlight it as "phase two - research needed".

Watch out

Assuming that if you've filled out one store page, the others will somehow sort themselves out. Treating rating and certification processes as a small formality rather than a schedule driver. And promising a multi-platform launch because it sounds impressive, without anyone owning the ongoing work of keeping several different store pages - and everything behind them - accurate, compliant and compelling.

Topic: .... Date: ....

Store Page Checklist (Example: Steam-like)

A Steam-like store page is your main wishlist engine before launch and your sales page after launch. It's not a bureaucratic form. It's a small, focused funnel: either it convinces people that "this is for me, now", or it quietly loses them.
You don't need a marketing team to make it work. You do need to know, for each element, what job it's doing.

The page as a small funnel
At the top: visuals and top-line text that decide whether players stay longer than three seconds. In the middle: description, screenshots and trailer that confirm (or break) the fantasy. At the bottom: price, tags, technical info and social proof that help players decide.

Walk through your page in that order and treat each element as a tool, not decoration.
Hero art / main capsule: This is what people see in carousels and "More Like This". It should show the core fantasy in one glance: genre, mood, point of view. If a stranger can't guess "what kind of game" this is from the image alone, the capsule is too vague or too focused on logo/typography.
Title and short description: Together they answer: What is this and why should I care? The first sentence of the short description should carry the hook: fantasy + core activity + twist. Cut buzzwords and empty claims ("immersive", "unique") that could fit any game.
Long description and features: This is where you make the promise concrete. Focus on what players actually do: loops, modes, progression, key systems. Use a small set of clear feature lines that describe experiences, not hype. "Run a chaotic restaurant kitchen under time pressure" is more useful than "deep simulation of culinary systems".
Screenshots: People scan screens much faster than text. Show real, readable gameplay: core loop, UI in context, key environments, a sense of progression or variety. Avoid grey-box shots, debug UI and concept art masquerading as in-game. If a screenshot would make players feel misled once they boot the game, drop it.
Trailer: On many pages, the trailer auto-plays by default. The first seconds must establish fantasy and basic gameplay, not just logos and slow logos. Structure matters: opening hook, core loop, variety, payoff. A random montage with fast cuts can excite you internally, but often leaves new players confused.
Tags, genres, categories: Tags tell both the platform and the player how to classify you. Use tags that your real audience expects and actually searches for. Over-claiming popular tags your game doesn't deliver on ("RPG", "horror", "roguelike") may help clicks today and hurt reviews and trust tomorrow.
System requirements and technical notes: Dry but important. They quietly answer: "Will this even run for me?" and "What's the input / connectivity reality?". If the game is controller-first, say it. If it requires a strong GPU or permanent internet, say it. Surprises here turn into refunds and negative reviews.

Quick best-practice lens
When reviewing your page, ask for each element:
- Is this communicating the current game, or an older internal version?
- Could this exact text or image describe three other games in the same genre?
- Do trailer, screenshots and text feel like they belong to the same product in tone and scope?

If the answer is "no" or "not really" too often, you don't need more elements, you need more coherence.

Try this
On the right-hand page, list the main elements of your store page in one column: hero art, short description, long description, screenshots, trailer, tags, features, system requirements.
Next to each, mark it as:
- Ready – we would be fine shipping this as-is.
- Decent placeholder – not final, but honest and consistent.
- Risky placeholder – outdated, misleading, or clearly too weak.

For every "risky placeholder", write one short line: what must change for it to become "ready" (for example: "new captures after UI overhaul", "rewrite first sentence to show fantasy", "replace mockup art with real gameplay"). This becomes a mini-backlog for improving wishlist and conversion without needing a full marketing plan.

Watch out
Treating the store page as a one-time submission task, not a living asset worth iterating. Leaving "temporary" screenshots, capsules or trailers online long after the game has changed. And letting different elements sell different games: cosy sim in the text, hardcore challenge in the trailer, chaotic meme screenshots in the gallery. When the page tells three stories at once, most players simply decide the game probably isn't for them and move on.

Topic: .... Date: ....

Wishlist Drivers & Pre-launch Tactics (1)

On Steam and similar platforms, wishlists are your main pre-launch signal. They don't equal sales, but they tell you whether strangers see your game, understand it, and care enough to save it. Before release, most of your visible activity should either bring people to the store page or give them a reason to click "Add to wishlist".
Here we use Steam as the main reference, but the logic applies to any store with a "follow / notify me" mechanic.

What a wishlist is really telling you
Think of wishlists as the result of a simple chain:
People first see your game somewhere. Some of them click through to your store page. A fraction of those decide to wishlist.
Roughly: ***impressions → visits → wishlists → later purchases***.

You can't control the whole chain, but you can influence:

- How many people who see you actually visit (your click-through reality, even if you don't have exact CTR numbers).
- How many visitors feel confident enough to wishlist (wishlists per visit, even tracked very roughly).

Watching only total wishlists hides the useful part. What matters is whether changes to your page or tactics make more visitors say "yes, I'll save this" instead of closing the tab.

Three main groups of drivers
Without a UA budget, almost all realistic wishlist tactics fall into three buckets: on the store page, outside the store, and inside your community.

On the store page is the foundation. If the page is weak, every tactic mostly wastes visibility. Before chasing tricks, make sure your fantasy and hook are clear in the title, short description and hero art; screenshots and trailer show real, current gameplay; tags and features match what the game actually is. Then create small "moments" that justify new visits: a visual refresh, a new trailer, a feature pass that changes how the game looks or plays. Every meaningful update is a reason to talk about the project again and send people to a more convincing page.

Outside the store you're looking for visibility spikes that don't require ad spend. Typical options include digital festivals and showcases, a public or time-limited demo, organic coverage from creators who like your genre, and consistent posting on one or two social channels instead of trying to be everywhere. All of these work better if the store page is already strong and the build you show is stable enough not to scare people away.

Inside your community you turn interested people into early advocates. That can be a Discord server, a simple mailing list, or a small playtest group. The tactic is straightforward: give them something to try, ask for feedback, and remind them to wishlist if they enjoy the direction. Community wishlists are usually "cheaper" than those from broad awareness, but they depend on you showing up regularly, answering questions and being transparent about progress.

"Why wishlist now?" vs "maybe later"
The key pre-launch question is: what changes for a player if they wishlist today instead of doing nothing?
If the honest answer is "not much", your messaging will feel like begging for support. Better answers include: they will see when the demo goes live, they won't miss launch discounts, they get to follow visible milestones, or they feel involved in shaping the game. Whenever you plan a pre-launch activity, ask how it gives players a concrete reason to act now rather than "when it's out someday".

Minimum realistic tactics
For most teams, the realistic minimum looks like this: a clear, up-to-date store page; participation in at least one relevant festival or event; a demo or public playtest round at some point before launch; and one focused channel where you consistently show progress and occasionally push people toward the store link. That alone is already work. Adding more tactics only makes sense once this baseline is handled with care.
You can still be data-aware without a full analytics setup. Even simple observations like "after the demo weekend we saw more visits and more wishlists per day than before" help you connect actions to outcomes and avoid working purely on gut feeling.

Topic: .... Date: ....

Wishlist Drivers & Pre-launch Tactics (2)

Try this

On the right-hand page, draw three headings: Store page, Outside, Community. Under each, write one to three actions you can realistically execute in the next 4–6 weeks without any paid marketing. Keep them small and concrete, for example: “refresh screenshots after art pass”, “apply to one festival or event”, “run a weekend playtest and post a wishlist reminder to participants”.

Next to each action, note what you expect it to influence: more visits, better wishlists per visit, or both. After you do it, check your store page stats for a few days and jot down what actually happened. The goal is to build the habit of linking tactics to numbers, even if the numbers are small.

Watch out

Copying complex AAA pre-launch plans when you don’t have their budgets or audience. Sending players to a weak or outdated store page and assuming the festival was “bad” when results disappoint. Spamming social channels with vague hype and no store link. And, above all, obsessing over ever more tactics while ignoring the simplest bottleneck: when someone finally lands on your page, do they understand what the game is and why it’s worth a spot on their wishlist right now?

Topic: .... Date: ....

Launch Readiness – Store & Comms Checklist

A "gold" build is not the same as being ready to launch. On Steam and similar platforms, launch is a coordinated moment: build, store page, price and regions, achievements, and communication all landing in a clear window. If any of those is missing, you don't have a launch – you have an uploaded executable.

What players will see on day one

Start from the outside in: if a stranger opens your store page at launch, does it show the real, current game?

By this point, your hero art, short and long description, screenshots, trailer, tags and feature bullets should match the launch experience, not an old pitch. If you changed art style, removed a mode, cut a major feature or improved UI, the page must reflect that before release.

If you support multiple languages, at least your key store texts should be final and checked in those languages. A polished build with half-baked, machine-like store text screams "unfinished".

If you work with a publisher or partner, add one more requirement: their approvals for copy and assets are already done. Launch-readiness includes their green light, not only yours.

Technical and commercial readiness

"Build ready" means the game runs and passes your tests. "Launch ready" means it also passes the platform's expectations and is configured for real customers.

For a Steam-like launch, that usually means:

- A release branch that has been tested as a release branch, not just "it ran on dev".
- Product configuration checked: app, depots and branches set correctly; achievements and other platform features configured or explicitly not used; demo/prologue entries (if any) aligned with the main product.
- Pricing and regions set and verified: base price, regional equivalents, any launch discounts scheduled, and no missing territories or accidental zero-price markets.

If other platforms are involved, all age ratings, tax and certification steps must be passed and visible in the dashboards, not "submitted, we hope it's fine". A lot of "last-minute launch crises" are just admin work postponed for too long.

Minimal communication plan

Even a small launch needs a minimal plan for who hears about it and when. At this stage you should know:

- The exact date and time you aim to go live on your main platform.
- Which basic channels you will use: at least a store news post, your core social channel(s), maybe Discord and a mailing.
- The rough content of those posts: what you're announcing, where the link goes, whether you mention a roadmap, discount, or demo.

You don't need a cinematic campaign. You do need to avoid the anti-pattern where the game silently releases, the team is still firefighting on the build, and nobody on your own channels mentions that the game is out for several hours.

If a publisher or partner is involved, they may also have their own posts, but those don't replace your direct communication with players.

Simple status pass instead of gut feeling

Treat launch readiness like a short checklist, not a feeling of "we're probably okay".

For each of these areas: Store page content, Pricing & regions, Release build & branches, Achievements / platform features, Localised store descriptions, Launch day communication (date, time, channels).

ask yourself honestly: Green (ready), Yellow (at risk), or Red (not ready).

Green means you could go live tomorrow without embarrassment. Yellow means "we think it'll be fine, but there are known issues". Red means something fundamental is missing (no final price, no tested release branch, store page lying about features).

Try this

On the right-hand page, recreate the list above as a small table with two columns: Area and Status. For every item marked At risk or Not ready, write one concrete next step, not a vague wish: "update long description after cutting co-op", "double-check regional prices", "prepare three short launch posts for Steam News, Discord and main social channel".

If several critical items are still red close to the planned date, that's not bad luck – it's a signal. Adjust the launch plan instead of hoping players won't notice the gaps.

Watch out

Equating "we have a build" with "we're ready to launch". Leaving the store page in an early state that describes a different game. Forgetting about regional pricing, age ratings or localisation until it's too late. And going live quietly, with no coordinated announcement, then being surprised that wishlists barely converted and early reviews complain about issues you could have addressed before the big red button.

Topic: .... Date: ....

Post-launch 30/60/90 Days – Focus Map

Launch is not the finish line. For most premium games, the first 90 days split into three phases: stabilise, consolidate, then decide how far you want to push the game. If you treat it all as one big "do everything now", the team burns out and the game drifts.
This page suggests a simple frame: 30 / 60 / 90 days crossed with three lanes – Tech & Bugs, Content & Balance, Marketing & Community. In each window you pick a few priorities instead of trying to move everything at once.

First 30 days – stabilise and listen
The first month is about trust. Players decide whether your game is something to recommend, refund or forget.

In Tech & Bugs, the focus is firefighting: crashes, progress loss, broken saves, serious performance issues, blockers in key missions. Hotfixes are fine, but they still need basic testing. You're not polishing; you're making sure people can actually play.
In Content & Balance, you mostly listen. Collect patterns from reviews, support tickets, forums, Discord: repeated pain points around difficulty spikes, grind, confusing systems, missing quality-of-life. Avoid redesigning core mechanics based on a few loud voices.
In Marketing & Community, the job is showing up and being clear. Acknowledge known issues, share what you're fixing next, and avoid defensive arguments. Even a small, honest post explaining priorities beats silence or fragmented replies.

Days 31–60 – consolidate and adjust
The second month is for consolidation: moving from emergency mode to planned updates.

In Tech & Bugs, this is when you ship a more structured patch: performance improvements, controller or UI fixes, stability for edge cases that didn't block everyone but annoyed many. The goal is fewer surprises and fewer "same bug, new report".
In Content & Balance, you implement targeted changes based on the patterns you saw: clearer tutorials, softened spikes, reduced busywork, a few quality-of-life upgrades. If you have data skills, use basic metrics (completion, retention, playtime) to confirm what reviews already hint at. If not, organised reading of feedback is still valuable.
In Marketing & Community, you highlight that the game is being improved, not abandoned. Readable patch notes, a short summary post or trailer for major updates, and updated store text or screenshots if the game has visibly changed. This is also a good moment to review your review score trend and adjust expectations.

Days 61–90 – choose the longer arc
By the third month, you have a clearer picture: performance, reception, team energy. The focus shifts to choosing a path, not just "more patches".

In Tech & Bugs, you handle remaining high-impact problems and focus on avoiding regressions. Massive refactors or risky overhauls are usually safer after you've decided how long and how big the game's support tail will be.
In Content & Balance, you decide whether to commit to meaningful new content (modes, levels, missions, systems) or aim for a smaller, polished package with occasional fixes. That decision should balance both feedback and resources: what players are asking for, what actually moves the needle, and what the team can realistically deliver.
In Marketing & Community, either you start framing a modest roadmap (even a short one) or you shift to less frequent, more substantial updates. This is also a good time to look at similar games: which ones are still talked about months after launch, and what kind of ongoing support they chose.

Try this
On the right-hand page, draw a simple grid: rows **0–30**, **31–60**, **61–90** days; columns **Tech & Bugs**, **Content & Balance**, **Marketing & Community**.
For each time window, write one or two priorities per column, maximum. Keep them general, for example: "stability hotfixes", "first QoL/balance patch", "define and announce roadmap". If your team can work with data, note next to each period which signals you'll check (review trends, crash rate, wishlists, playtime). If not, commit to at least reading a sample of reviews and threads around each milestone.
The point is not to fill every box. The point is to see, on one page, what you're actually focusing on.

Watch out
Staying in permanent launch crisis mode and never shifting gears. Jumping into big DLC plans while the base game is still unstable. Letting the loudest comments on social channels steer your roadmap without checking broader patterns. And trying to grow, fix and reinvent the game all at once, instead of deliberately moving from "put out fires" to "improve" to "choose the long-term path" over those first 90 days.

Topic: .... Date: ....

Monetization Models Summary

Monetization is not there to "squeeze" players. It's how you connect the value of your game with the reality of your team and your audience. For most small and medium PC/console teams, the default is still premium – one price for the full game – with a few possible layers on top. F2P exists, but it behaves like a different business entirely.
This page is a quick map, not a full economy design guide.

Premium – one price, full game
How it works: players pay once, get the complete experience. You might still patch and add small free updates, but the core promise is "you bought the game".
Typical pluses: simple to explain, widely accepted, easier to scope and test. Good fit for contained single-player experiences and games without strong long-term loops.
Typical minuses: revenue is front-loaded around launch and discounts; pressure to cram everything into the base game; harder to justify heavy ongoing work unless the game really breaks out.

Premium + DLC / expansions
How it works: premium base game plus paid content chunks later – new campaigns, maps, systems, story arcs.
Pluses: extends the life of a successful title, lets you grow the world where there is demand, can fund additional development without starting a new IP. Players who loved the base game often welcome "more of that".
Minuses: assumes a sizable, engaged player base; production and QA cost for each drop; risk of cutting base content "to sell later" if you aren't disciplined; fragmented expectations ("which version should I buy?").
Good fit when your fantasy and systems naturally support more stories, regions or challenges without re-inventing the whole game.

Premium + cosmetic / small packs
How it works: base game plus optional cosmetics, skin packs, OSTs, "supporter" bundles or small add-ons that don't split the player base.
Pluses: extra revenue from most engaged fans; doesn't usually break balance; can be scoped relatively small. Works best when cosmetics are visible and meaningful inside the game fantasy.
Minuses: easy to drift into clutter and cynicism ("why is this not just included?"); UI and store integration takes time; needs care not to look like a mobile shop bolted onto a premium title.
Use this when you can offer items that feel like expression and affection for the game, not locks on basic enjoyment.

Seasonal passes / light live-ops on top of premium
How it works: time-limited progression tracks, challenges and mostly cosmetic rewards layered on a game people play repeatedly.
Pluses: can give structure to ongoing updates; players who are already engaged get reasons to return; revenue becomes less spiky if done well.
Minuses: requires reliable live-ops capacity, calendar discipline, and a core loop that naturally brings people back. In a finite single-player experience, a battle pass usually feels artificial and exhausting.
Only consider this if your game is already built around replay, progression and recurring engagement – not as a way to "add live service" at the end.

F2P – a different business
If your studio is not built around F2P from day one, treat it as "out of scope" rather than a late pivot.

Try this
On the right-hand page, write the name of your project and pick one main and one optional secondary model from above (for example: "Premium" + "DLC later" or "Premium" + "Cosmetic packs").
For each chosen model, jot down three short lines:

- How it actually works in your game.
- Why it fits (or potentially clashes with) your fantasy and core loop.
- What it demands from your team after launch.

If you can't answer those without hand-waving, mark that model as "nice idea, not core".

Watch out
Designing your game around a fashionable model that fights your fantasy. Bolting passes or micro-stores onto a finite story just because "everyone does it". Underestimating how much ongoing work even "light" post-launch monetization needs. And changing models mid-development without revisiting whether your game, your audience and your team are actually built to support that choice.

Topic: .... Date: ....

Basic Marketing Funnel – From Awareness to Retention (1)

Marketing is just a way of moving people from "never heard of it" to "I bought it and might come back". On Steam and similar platforms, that path is surprisingly simple: people discover your game, get interested enough to open the store page, decide whether to buy or wishlist, and then either disappear or stick around.
This page uses a basic four-step funnel – awareness → interest → purchase → retention – as a practical lens, not a theory lesson.

A simple four-step funnel (basic on purpose)

Awareness – "I've seen this game somewhere."
Players notice your game in a festival, on social media, in a creator's video, in "More Like This", or in a friend's message. They don't know details yet; they just recognise the name, capsule or vibe.

Interest – "I want to know more."
Some of those people click through. On Steam, that means visits to your store page. At this stage, they scan your capsule, trailer, screenshots and short description to decide if it fits their taste.

Purchase (or wishlist) – "I'm willing to commit."
Here they either buy, add to wishlist, follow, or drop off. For unreleased games, wishlists and follows are the main "yes" signal. For released games, it's actual purchases – often influenced by price, discount, and early reviews.

Retention – "I keep playing or stay connected."
After buying, players either bounce quickly or stick around: finishing the game, returning for updates, leaving reviews, talking about it, recommending it. For a premium game, retention also includes people who don't play daily but stay in your orbit (Discord, mailing list, store follows) for future content or games.
You can add more nuance, but this basic version is enough to organise your thinking.

Minimum actions for each stage

For small and medium teams, a realistic minimum is to do something deliberate at each step, mostly with organic tools.

Awareness
At minimum, pick one or two main awareness sources you can actually support: a couple of relevant festivals; one or two social channels; a handful of creators who genuinely like your genre. You don't need to be everywhere; you need a few repeatable places where new people can discover you.

Interest
Here your store page does the heavy lifting. The minimum is: clear fantasy and hook in the first line of text, honest screenshots and railer that show the real loop, tags that match what the game is. Every awareness push should point to a page that actually helps people decide, not to an old placeholder.

Purchase
For unreleased games, the minimum is a visible wishlist button, a clear call to action in your description and posts ("add to wishlist if it looks like your thing"), and a plan for launch pricing and discount. For released games, that plus sensible discount participation and making sure the page reflects recent improvements. Paid campaigns can sit on top of this, but they don't replace it.
Retention
The minimum here is to not disappear. Show up with readable patch notes, occasional updates, and a place where players can talk to you (Discord, Steam forum, social). If your game supports replay or future content, tell people what you're realistically planning next instead of going silent.

Using data (when you can – and why it's worth learning)
Even basic numbers can make this funnel less vague. On Steam, you can approximate:

- Awareness → interest: how many people who saw you somewhere ended up visiting your page.
- Interest → purchase/wishlist: how many visitors actually wishlist or buy.
- Purchase → retention: how long people play, whether reviews mention quitting early or staying engaged.

If your team knows how to read these signals, use them. If not, it's still worth slowly learning – even rough trends ("we updated the page and wishlists per day went up") are better than guessing. Just don't wait for perfect analytics before doing the obvious minimum.

Topic: .... Date: ....

Basic Marketing Funnel – From Awareness to Retention (2)

Try this

On the right-hand page, draw four boxes: Awareness, Interest, Purchase, Retention.
Inside each box, write 2–3 channels or actions you are already using (for example: "festival X, Twitter" under Awareness; "Steam page, trailer" under Interest). Then mark, in simple words, which stage feels weakest today and why.
Below the weakest stage, write one small action you can take in the next month to strengthen it. Keep it realistic: "improve first two screenshots", "apply to one festival", "write clearer patch notes", not "become viral everywhere".

Watch out

Obsessing over awareness (more trailers, more posts, more festivals) while your store page still confuses visitors. Focusing only on launch purchases and ignoring whether people actually play and recommend the game. Treating retention as a free bonus instead of the thing that turns buyers into long-term fans. And expecting one strong stage in the funnel to compensate for another that you've never really addressed.

Topic: .... Date: ....

Key Messages – What Your Game Is Really Saying

Every game tells a story long before players press "Start". Store pages, trailers, screenshots, social posts, devlogs, even patch notes – together they create a few core ideas that people remember. Those are your key messages, whether you plan them or not. This page is about making those messages explicit and consistent, so you don't accidentally sell a different game every month.

Why key messages matter

Most players will only ever hear a handful of things about your game. They might remember the fantasy ("chaotic cooking in a tiny kitchen"), the core experience ("short, replayable missions"), who it's for ("people who like management games but don't want hardcore sims"), and a "why now" hook ("perfect for quick sessions after work").

If those four ideas keep changing between your store page, trailers and social posts, players feel something is off. They might not articulate it, but they sense confusion and move on.

You don't need a big brand document. You do need a small, shared set of sentences that everyone on the team can use and adapt.

A simple player-facing template

For this notebook, keep it basic and focused on players. Use this four-line template as your starting point:

1. Fantasy – what world or role you offer.
2. Core experience – what players actually do most of the time.
3. For whom – who will feel "this is for me".
4. Why now – why someone should care today, not "someday".

For example, when you write your own version, think along the lines of:

- Fantasy: "Run a tiny but chaotic restaurant kitchen where everything can go wrong."
- Core experience: "Cook, plate and serve orders under time pressure while managing a growing menu."
- For whom: "For players who enjoy management and sim games but prefer short, focused sessions over endless grinding."
- Why now: "Perfect if you want a fresh, small-scope kitchen game you can pick up after work without committing to a huge campaign."

Write it in your voice, not in template language, but keep the structure. This becomes the backbone for how you talk about the game everywhere players see you.

One core, different wrappers

You can adapt the same key messages for different audiences without rewriting the story every time. For players, you speak in terms of fantasy, actions and feelings. For business partners or press, you might frame the same ideas in terms of genre position, target segment and differentiators. The important part: the core doesn't change. If your player-facing message says "cosy, low-pressure experience", your "for business" version should not suddenly sell "hardcore competitive play". You can shift angle and vocabulary, but not the underlying promise. When you feel tempted to change the story, ask whether the game itself actually changed, or you're just reacting to the latest trend or comment thread.

Keeping messages consistent over time

Key messages are not a prison. They can and should evolve if the game genuinely shifts direction. But changes need to be deliberate and explained, not random swings.

When something major changes – for example, you cut co-op, add a strong roguelite loop, or reposition from "chill" to "challenging" – revisit your four sentences. Update them once, then update your main public surfaces: store page, trailer copy, social bios or pinned posts. Tell players what changed and why, instead of silently drifting.

If the only reason you're rewriting messages is that you're bored of saying the same thing, that's a trap. Players are just arriving; for them this is the first time, not the fiftieth.

Try this

On the right-hand page, write the name of your current project at the top. Under it, use four short lines:

Fantasy: , Core experience: , For whom: , Why now:

Fill each with one clear, player-facing sentence. Then, underneath, write a second, shorter version of the same four lines as you would say them in a meeting with a platform rep or press – same meaning, slightly different framing.

Finally, circle any words that feel vague ("innovative", "deep", "immersive"). Replace them with concrete images or actions. If you can't, that's a sign the idea isn't clear enough yet.

Watch out

Chasing every new trend by rewriting what your game "really is" every few weeks. Letting store pages, trailers and social posts describe three different products. Hiding big changes in direction instead of updating your core story. And assuming that players will "just get it" without you ever sitting down to decide, in a few sentences, what you actually want the game to say to them.

Topic: .... Date: ....

Asset Requests for Marketing – What They Need

Marketing can only work with what it actually has in hand. If your team "will make the trailer later" or "still tweaks the logo", you're silently blocking all promotion. For small and medium teams doing marketing internally, the goal is not a perfect cinematic package. The goal is a small, reliable set of assets that arrives early enough and is stable enough to build around. This page helps you name those assets and decide who does what, by when.

Why asset planning matters

Every marketing beat – announcing the game, joining a festival, sending keys to creators, updating the store page – consumes assets. You need key art for capsules and thumbnails, a logo that works on light and dark backgrounds, screenshots that match current visuals, a trailer, some short clips or B-roll, maybe a few images tailored for social posts or influencer kits.

If you only think about these when a deadline appears ("festival wants a trailer next week"), you end up rushing, compromising or saying "no" to good opportunities. Planning a small asset set early gives you options later.

Start from a realistic baseline. You can always add more formats and versions as the game grows.

A minimal asset set for small/medium teams

For most premium PC/console projects, an internal "version 1" list looks like this in practice:

- Key art and logo that define the visual identity and can be reused across capsules, thumbnails and banners.
- Store capsules / hero images in a few common ratios, derived from that key art, not random crops.
- Screenshots that show real, current gameplay: core loop, UI, mood, a sense of variety.
- One main trailer that explains the fantasy and core experience within seconds, plus a handful of short clips or raw footage you can cut down for social posts or creator use.
- Basic influencer/media kit: a small folder with logo variants, key art, clean screenshots and a short text summary of the game.

Formats, resolutions and exact specs vary per platform and will change over time. Treat technical details as a checklist you look up before exporting, not as something you memorise. What matters here is that someone owns creating and updating these items.

As your game grows or gains a publisher, this list can expand into more versions: localised logos or title cards, platform-specific banners, more trailers, event-specific key visuals. Start small and solid; let it grow intentionally instead of chaotically.

Assets are needed earlier than you think

Marketing moments often happen before the game looks "finished" to you. Festivals, platform pitches, first creator outreach, even your own announcement all need visuals and video that you feel safe putting in front of strangers.

That means you need to lock at least some asset plans weeks or months earlier than your gut says. If you want a trailer for an event, you need capture windows and shot lists before that. If you want creators to cover your game at launch, you need a clean kit for them ready ahead of keys.

Waiting for "perfect" usually means you end up with rushed, inconsistent assets – or no visibility at all.

Try this

On the right-hand page, draw three columns: Asset, Who, Deadline / Status.

In the Asset column, list your minimal set: key art + logo, store capsules, screenshots, main trailer, short clips/B-roll, basic influencer kit. In the Who column, write the name or role responsible. In the Deadline / Status column, note either a clear date or a short status like "concept approved", "needs capture after new UI", "ready for export per platform specs".

Then put a small star next to three assets that are critical for starting wishlist-building and basic promotion. These are your non-negotiables; everything else is follow-up. If any starred item has no owner or no date, that is a hidden risk.

Watch out

Assuming assets will "come together" naturally without clear owners. Handing marketing work to "future you" while also expecting strong pre-launch results. Delivering key visuals, screenshots or trailers at the last minute, leaving no time for feedback or iteration. And forgetting that for people outside the team, your assets are the game until they actually play it – rough, inconsistent or outdated visuals make the whole project look less ready than it might be in reality.

Topic: .... Date: ....

Working with Influencers & Creators

For many PC/console games, creators on YouTube, Twitch and short-form platforms are the first "review" players see. A good video from the right channel can do more than weeks of your own posts. But creators are not a vending machine: you don't put in a key and get guaranteed coverage out.

This page is about treating them as partners: picking the right people and giving them what they need to make a good piece of content.

Different creators, different needs

Creators work in different formats: edited reviews, Let's Plays, long streams, short highlights. Their workflows differ, but they usually want:

A stable build that won't crash on stream, A clear, short explanation of what the game is and why it's interesting, Assets to make thumbnails and intros (logo, key art, clean screenshots, maybe a clip), Guidance plus freedom: ideas on what might be fun to show, but no script.

Big channels run on tight schedules; smaller and mid-size ones are more flexible but flooded with requests. In both cases, respect and clarity stand out.

Prepare before you send a single key

Before you reach out, make sure you have:

A short pitch: 2–3 lines in normal language explaining the fantasy, core experience and why it could fit their audience. No buzzword salad.

A creator-friendly build: stable, with basic options (volume, keybinds, difficulty) and a path to something interesting within a reasonable time. If your early game is slow, consider ways for preview builds to reach "the fun part" faster.

A small asset pack: logo (preferably on transparent background), key art, a few clean, UI-visible screenshots, optionally one or two short raw clips of real gameplay.

A tiny FAQ note: length, controller support, content caveats, embargo info, monetisation/VOD policy. Put it in a short readme or a simple page you can link.

If you don't have this, you're probably too early for outreach.

Choosing who to contact

For small and medium teams without an agency, it's better to go narrow and relevant than to mail a hundred random channels. Look for creators who:

Already play games in or near your genre, Sometimes cover smaller or indie titles, not only blockbusters, Have active comments and viewers that match your target players.

Don't chase size alone. A mid-size creator whose audience loves your niche is often more valuable than a huge variety channel where your game will be one more upload people skip.

Be clear that coverage is voluntary. A key is an invitation, not payment.

How to reach out (and follow up)

Keep your initial message short and human:

One line about who you are and what the game is, One line about why you thought of this creator, What you're offering: key, asset pack, FAQ link, relevant dates (launch, demo, update), A simple ask: if it fits their audience, you'd be happy if they considered covering it.

Expect many no-replies. A single polite follow-up is fine; pushing is not. When someone does make content about your game, show up: thank them, consider sharing the video/stream if it fits your channels, answer questions in comments if appropriate, take notes on what worked. Over time, you're building a small circle of creators who "get" your games.

Paid campaigns, if you ever use them, work better when this basic relationship mindset is already in place.

Try this

On the right-hand page, first write down five things you can offer creators besides a key – for example: early access to updates, dev Q&A, featuring their videos in your community, exclusive screenshots or concept art, or participation in a feedback session.

Then list three creators whose channels align with your target audience. For each, jot a single sentence: "Why would their viewers care about this game?" If you can't answer that clearly, don't pitch them yet.

Watch out

Treating creators as free ad slots instead of people with their own brand and constraints. Sending unstable builds and being surprised when bugs end up in the video. Copy-pasting the same generic email to dozens of channels. And disappearing after launch, instead of nurturing a few long-term relationships that might matter even more for your next game than for this one.

Topic: ....

Date: ....

Patch Notes Style – Talking About Changes

Patch notes are often the only "story" many players ever read about your game after launch. They can reassure people that the project is alive, explain why things feel different, and show that you understand what matters to your audience. Or they can be a wall of technical noise nobody finishes.
This page treats patch notes as communication first, not as a raw log of everything you changed in the build.

Patch notes as a player-facing story of the update
Every update answers three questions for players:
What changed that I will notice? Why did you change it? Should I come back and play again?
If your notes only list internal ticket IDs and "minor fixes", none of those questions are answered. On the other hand, if you oversell tiny tweaks as "huge updates", trust erodes.
Think of each patch as a short story: title, a few highlights, then details in a structure that respects players' time.

A simple structure that works for most games
You don't need a fancy format. You do need a consistent one. A simple template:

1. **Title and short intro:** One clear line: "Update 1.1 – Performance improvements and new challenges." Follow with 1–3 sentences explaining the purpose of the patch in plain language.
2. **Highlights:** A small section that surfaces the 3–5 changes most players will care about: new content, major balance shifts, big performance wins, key quality-of-life upgrades. This is the "headline" for people who will not read further.
3. **Gameplay and content changes:** Group changes by area (modes, levels, weapons, economy, enemies, etc.). Use short, direct lines that describe effects, not internal implementation. Explain intent when something might be controversial: "We reduced X to make Y more viable."
4. **Quality-of-life and UX:** Separate from pure balance: menus, controls, UI clarity, accessibility, small conveniences. These often matter disproportionately to day-to-day enjoyment and are worth calling out.
5. **Bug fixes:** Most players skim here, but it still matters. Avoid internal jargon; phrase fixes in terms of what was broken from a player's perspective: "Fixed a bug where...".
6. **Known issues / next steps:** If there are significant problems you're aware of but haven't fixed yet, acknowledge them briefly and state whether you're investigating or have a planned fix window. Manage expectations without promising miracles.

This basic shape can flex to fit small hotfixes or larger updates, but keeping the order consistent helps players orient quickly.

Style and tone: clear, honest, human
The "right" tone depends on your game and audience. Some communities enjoy a light, humorous voice; others prefer very neutral patch notes. Whatever you choose, a few principles are universal:

- Lead with clarity. Put important information in simple sentences before you add flavour.
- Avoid deep technical jargon. It's fine to mention performance or memory, but don't copy engine changelogs.
- Explain intent for big changes. A short "we did this because..." can turn anger into understanding, even if players disagree.
- Own your mistakes. If you broke something in a previous patch, acknowledge it without defensiveness and explain the fix.

Your goal is for a player skimming the notes to understand how their experience will change and to feel that there are competent humans on the other side.

Try this
On the right-hand page, take your last patch notes (even if they were just an internal list) and rewrite them using the structure above.
First, write a one-line title and a 2–3 sentence intro that explains the purpose of the update. Then, list 3–5 highlights you want players to notice. Below, group the remaining changes into "Gameplay & Content", "Quality-of-life & UX", "Bug fixes", and optionally "Known issues".
When you're done, mark any lines that still sound like internal tickets ("Fixed issue #1234") and rewrite them from a player's point of view. That rewrite is usually where the communication actually happens.

Watch out
Dumping raw Jira change lists into your patch notes and calling it a day. Hiding major nerfs or removals in the middle of a "misc fixes" paragraph. Writing clickbait titles for tiny updates. And never explaining why you changed something that players clearly cared about, forcing them to reverse-engineer your intent from a long, unstructured wall of text.

Topic: .... Date: ....

Community Touchpoints – Where You Actually Show Up

Your "community" is not an abstract blob. It's specific places where players see you, talk to you and talk about you: store forums, in-game feedback, Discord, social channels, review sections, maybe a subreddit or a small fan group somewhere. Trying to be everywhere usually means you end up nowhere in a meaningful way. For a small or medium team without a full-time community manager, the goal is to pick a few touchpoints and actually show up there.

Fewer channels, clearer expectations

It's tempting to open every possible channel at launch: forums, Discord, three socials, multiple languages. Most teams don't have the capacity to keep that alive.

A more honest approach is:

- Choose 2–3 primary touchpoints where you will be present and responsive.
- Treat everything else as listen-only or "we might occasionally post here".

For example, your primary touchpoints might be: store community hub / forum, one real-time channel (Discord or similar), and one main social feed. Reviews and external forums still matter, but you treat them as places to monitor, not to manage.

For each chosen channel, decide what it's for: bug reports and support, announcements, discussion, sharing fan content, feedback on updates, or a mix. A channel without a purpose quickly becomes noise.

Who answers, how fast, and in what tone

Players don't just care where you show up; they care how you behave when you're there.

For each primary touchpoint, get clear on three basics:

- Who responds: which person or role owns this channel. "Everyone" usually means "no-one".
- How fast: what is a realistic response window (for example, "we try to reply to most posts within 24–48 hours on weekdays").
- What tone: more formal and concise, or more relaxed and chatty – as long as it fits your game and audience.

You don't need rigid "SLAs", but you do need shared expectations inside the team. Otherwise one person writes long, friendly essays, another writes two-word replies, and players feel like they're talking to strangers each time.

Showing up and listening

Community touchpoints are about both interaction and listening.

Interaction means replying to questions, acknowledging bugs, thanking people for feedback, and being visible around releases and patches. It does not mean arguing with every negative comment or trying to win debates.

Listening means deliberately scanning channels for patterns: recurring issues, common questions, surprising use cases, shifting sentiment around updates. You don't have to respond to everything you read, but you can't learn from conversations you never see.

A healthy practice is to turn what you hear into simple summaries for the team: "Top three issues mentioned this week", "Most liked features", "Things new players struggle with". That way community work feeds back into design and production instead of living in its own bubble.

Try this

On the right-hand page, draw a simple list of potential touchpoints for your current game: store forum, in-game feedback, Discord or chat server, one or two social channels, reviews, maybe an external forum or subreddit.

From that list, circle 2–3 channels you can realistically commit to as primary. Next to each circled channel, write three short lines:

- Who: the person/role responsible for checking and replying.
- How fast: a realistic response window.
- For what: the main purpose of this channel (support, announcements, discussion, etc.).

Below the list, note one or two places you will only monitor (for example, reviews or external forums) and write how often you plan to check them and what you'll look for (patterns, not individual drama).

Watch out

Opening every possible channel because "it's free", then leaving most of them half-dead. Treating player reports as an annoyance instead of input. Answering only on launch week and disappearing for months. And confusing "being online all the time" with having a clear, sustainable plan for where and how you actually show up for your community.

Topic: .... Date: ....

Review Monitoring – Feedback from Stores

Store reviews are a public mirror of your game. They're noisy, emotional, sometimes unfair – and still very useful if you treat them as signals, not a verdict on you as a person.
This page is about turning reviews from "scary number on the store" into a simple feedback loop.

More than a percentage
On PC/console stores (Steam, GOG, console stores and others) you usually see at least: average rating, number of reviews and how they change over time. Mobile stores are similar in spirit.
The score matters, but underneath you're really asking:
What do players think the game actually is? What do they praise by name? What keeps showing up as a pain point?
One person can own reading and summarising reviews, but the conclusions should be shared with design, tech and production. The goal isn't doomscrolling; it's feeding reality back into decisions.

Look for patterns, not drama
Reviews range from "best ever" to "worst ever". Individual extremes are mostly noise. Patterns are where value sits.
A simple approach:

1. Take a recent batch (for example 20–50 latest reviews).
2. For each, quickly tag in your notes: "praise – X", "complaint – Y", "mixed", "off-topic".
3. Group what repeats into three lists:

Things people like, Things they dislike, Themes that appear regardless of rating (for example, "great atmosphere, weak UX").
Ignore isolated rants that don't connect to anything else. Pay attention when very different players complain about the same issue.
If you have basic metrics (playtime, completion, crash rate), use them to check whether numbers support what reviews suggest. If not, reviews are still better than guessing.

Replying without making things worse
Your replies are also part of your public face. A few hard rules are worth stating clearly:

- Don't fight with reviewers. You almost never "win" that fight, and lots of people are watching.
- Respond selectively. Focus on reviews that highlight common problems, ask good questions or clearly misunderstand something important you can clarify.
- Be calm and factual. Thank them, address the point, don't get personal.
- Own real issues. If someone hits a known bug or design gap, acknowledge it and, if possible, point to a fix or a realistic plan.
- Don't overpromise. Avoid "we'll fix everything soon" unless you actually can.

On some platforms (especially mobile) replies may be your only direct contact with that player. Treat them like public support tickets.

Turning reviews into decisions
Monitoring only matters if it leads somewhere. A lightweight routine is enough:

- On a regular cadence (for example weekly in active periods), the person watching reviews writes a short summary:

3 key praises, 3 key complaints, 3 recurring themes.

- The team then marks each point as:

Actionable now (bugs, small QoL fixes), Needs design discussion, Not aligned with our goals (we understand, but we won't change this).

You'll never make everyone happy, but you can absolutely remove obvious friction that hurts both players and your long-term reputation.

Try this
On the right-hand page, imagine you just read the last 10 reviews on your main store.
Write three short lines:
People praise: , People complain about: , Most common themes:
When you have real data, repeat this exercise for real every few weeks. Compare how those three lines evolve after patches, price changes or updates.

Watch out
Staring only at the score and ignoring what people actually write. Reacting emotionally to every extreme review instead of looking at trends. Answering only praise and staying silent under well-written criticism. Or, on the other side, reading reviews obsessively but never turning them into a clear, prioritised list of changes the team will actually act on.

Topic: .... Date: ....

Competitor Watch – Simple Tracking

You don't make games in a vacuum. On PC and especially on Steam, your project lives next to a handful of other titles that your players already know. Watching those games with intent is not about obsession or copying. It's about understanding where your game sits in that landscape and what you can learn from neighbours who fight for the same attention.
This page keeps competitor tracking deliberately simple and narrow: a few close titles, a few observations, repeated over time.

Why bother watching competitors at all?
Your closest competitors are the games that:

- share a similar fantasy or theme,
- target the same kind of player,
- live in similar price and feature territory.

Those games silently set expectations for your audience. They influence what "normal" looks like for scope, pacing, visual quality, post-launch support and pricing. If you ignore them completely, you risk designing a game that feels strangely off – too bare for its price, too bloated for its niche, or positioned in a way that makes no sense from the outside.
Competitor watch is not there to decide your vision. It's there to help answer questions like:

- How does our pitch read next to theirs?
- What are they clearly doing better?
- What are they ignoring that we might lean into?

This is mostly about positioning: making sure your game has a clear, believable place in the minds of players who know those other titles.

A small, focused list
Instead of trying to watch the whole genre, pick 3–5 games that are genuinely close to your project. Think about what your future store visitors will see in "More Like This" or what your target players already have in their library.
For each chosen game, pay attention to:

- How they present themselves on their store page (fantasy, features, screenshots, trailer).
- How players talk about them in reviews (what people praise, what they complain about).
- How the game is maintained over time (updates, DLC, events) if it's already out.

At this stage, don't worry about complex tools. A simple table in your notebook is enough: one row per game, with space for "what they do well", "what they do differently from us", and "what we can learn".
If this habit proves useful, you can always scale later into spreadsheets or dedicated documents. Start with pen and paper.

Learning, not copying
There is a big difference between learning from a competitor and copying their features.
Learning is asking: "Why does this work for them?" and "Would it still work for our audience and our structure?" Copying is "They have crafting, so we add crafting", without understanding whether it fits your fantasy, your scope, or your players.
Feature lists on store pages are especially dangerous here. It's easy to start playing "checklist bingo": co-op, crafting, roguelite elements, talent trees, base building. If you blindly chase parity with a bigger game, you end up with a bloated project that delivers none of those elements especially well.

Use competitor tracking to clarify what you are not doing as much as what you are. Having a smaller, sharper promise can be more powerful than trying to look like a discount version of a much bigger title.

Try this
On the right-hand page, draw a simple table with four columns: Game, Does well, Does differently, What we learn.
Pick three games that are closest to your current project. For each:

- In "Does well", write what they are clearly nailing in the eyes of their players (not only what you personally like).
- In "Does differently", note how their positioning, scope or systems diverge from your game.
- In "What we learn", write one short line – either something to emulate in spirit, something to avoid, or something that helps you describe your own game more clearly.

Repeat this exercise occasionally as those games get updates, DLC or sequels. Over time, you'll get a clearer picture of how your project fits – and where it can stand out – without turning competitor watch into a full-time job.

Watch out
Treating competitor tracking as a shopping list of features you must match. Obsessing over other games' success or failures instead of focusing on your own players. Ignoring clear signals about positioning and scope because "we're different" in ways players don't see. And, above all, copying solutions you don't truly understand, then being surprised when they fail in a context where your game, your team and your audience are not the same.

Topic: .... Date: ....

Block F
Team & Communication

Topic: ....

Date: ....

Types of Meetings

In a 5–30 person team, meetings can keep a project aligned or quietly eat half of everyone's week. A meeting is just a tool: useful when it does a specific job, harmful when it replaces thinking, documentation or an honest "we don't know yet".
This page groups meetings into a few simple types. If a meeting doesn't clearly fit one of them, there's a good chance you don't need it.

1. Status / sync – "Are we on track?"
Purpose: Share what's going on and spot risks early.
Use when: You need the whole group to see the same picture: what's done, what's in progress, what's blocked. Short, regular, predictable (for example, a quick weekly sync).
Avoid when: You just want individual task updates you could read in the tracker. If people are reciting what's already written, you're wasting time. Status meetings are for exceptions and risks, not for reading the board aloud.

2. Planning – "What will we do next?"
Purpose: Decide what the team focuses on in the next chunk of time (week, sprint, milestone).
Use when: You have some input (backlog, roadmap, constraints) and need to agree as a group what makes sense now: priorities, scope, who takes what.
Avoid when: You haven't done basic prep. Planning without a rough backlog, capacity and constraints turns into a vague brainstorming session. Planning is about choices, not generating ideas from scratch.

3. Review / demo – "Did we build the right thing?"
Purpose: Look at real work together – builds, features, art – and check if it matches the intention.
Use when: There is something concrete to show: a playable build, a feature slice, concept pass, vertical slice. The goal is feedback against goals, not against personal taste only.
Avoid when: There is nothing to show yet. A review without a demo turns into another planning or status meeting. Better to postpone than pretend.

4. Problem-solving – "How do we fix this?"
Purpose: Unblock a specific issue that can't be resolved asynchronously: design conflict, technical constraint, scope trade-off.
Use when: You have a clearly defined problem, right people in the (virtual) room, and you're ready to make a decision or at least testable next step.
Avoid when: The problem is still fuzzy. If you can't summarise it in a few sentences beforehand, you're not ready. Don't invite a crowd to "figure out what the problem is" live if one or two people could clarify it first.

5. Direction / decision – "Which way are we going?"
Purpose: Take decisions that shape the project: vision, big features, scope cuts, dates, pricing.
Use when: The topic has been prepared: options, trade-offs, risks are known, and you need alignment plus a final call from the owner (director, lead, producer).
Avoid when: You hope the meeting itself will magically generate a decision without anyone willing to own it. Direction meetings need a clear decider; otherwise you just push the issue forward.

6. 1:1 – "How are we doing as people?"
Purpose: Maintain alignment and trust with individuals: feedback, growth, blockers, sanity check.
Use when: You're a lead/producer and want regular, private space with key people to talk about more than tasks.
Avoid when: You only use 1:1s as mini status meetings. If all you do is go through a task list, you could do it in the tracker.

Try this
On the right-hand page, list all recurring meetings in your project from the last two weeks. Next to each, write which type it should be (status, planning, review, problem-solving, direction, 1:1).
If any meeting doesn't fit, or tries to be three types at once, mark it with a question mark. Those are your first candidates to cancel, split, or redesign with a clearer purpose and smaller group.

Watch out
"Meetings for everything" because it feels safer than making a call. Status calls that repeat the task board. Reviews without anything to review. Problem-solving sessions where nobody owns the decision. And big mixed meetings that pretend to be status, planning and decision-making at the same time – and end up doing none of them well.

Topic: .... Date: ....

Meeting Agenda Template

A meeting without an agenda is just an expensive group chat. In a small or mid-sized team, every hour you pull people away from focused work has a cost. An agenda doesn't have to be a long document – it just needs to make clear why you're meeting, what you'll cover, and what decisions you want by the end.

This page gives you two tiny templates you can reuse: one for short syncs, one for bigger meetings. If you can't fill one of them in a couple of minutes, you probably shouldn't have the meeting.

Light agenda (30 minutes or less)

Use this for quick syncs, small planning huddles or focused problem-solving with a few people.

Before the meeting, write:

1. **Goal (1 sentence):** "By the end of this meeting we want to: …" (If you have no clear goal, cancel or turn it into an async update.)
2. **Timebox:** "Max 30 minutes, end by HH:MM." (This forces you to prioritise instead of wandering.)
3. **Topics (3 or fewer):** Each topic gets: a short name and an owner. For example:

"Build issues – Alex"; "Scope for tutorial – Martha"

4. **Expected outcome:** One line: "Decisions / clarifications we need:" with 1–3 bullets.

That's it. The light agenda fits in a chat message or a short note in your tracker. Send it ahead of time or put it in the calendar description so people know why they're there.

Heavy agenda (60–90 minutes, bigger decisions)

Use this for planning sessions, reviews, direction/decision meetings with more people and more impact.

Before the meeting, write:

1. **Purpose and context (2–3 sentences)**

What this meeting is about, why now, and what changed since last time. This keeps old topics from sneaking back in.

2. **Max duration and hard stop**

"60 minutes, hard stop at HH:MM." If you can't fit the topics, cut them. Don't just extend by default.

3. **Agenda with owners**

A short list, ordered by priority, for example:

   a. "Review current milestone risks – lead producer (15 min)"
   b. "Decide on tutorial scope cut – design + tech (25 min)"
   c. "Next steps / assignments – all (10 min)"

4. **Decisions we must leave with**

A small section: "We must decide today:" followed by 2–4 concrete items. If you can't name them, you don't need this meeting yet.

5. **Parking lot**

A simple note: "Out-of-scope topics go to parking lot." During the call, anything off-topic gets parked and handled later, instead of derailing the main goal.

If you can't fill this in quickly, do more prep or postpone. A vague agenda almost guarantees a vague outcome.

A tiny summary at the end

Agenda is "before", but you also need a minimal "after". At the end of any meeting longer than a quick check-in, take 2–3 minutes for a verbal and written recap:

- Decisions: what did we actually decide?
- Owners: who is responsible for each follow-up?
- Deadlines: by when?

One person writes these three lines in a visible place (tracker, doc, meeting note). Without this step, even a good agenda doesn't prevent deja-vu meetings later.

Try this

Take your next planned meeting and write either the light or heavy agenda using the templates above. If you struggle to define the goal or the "must decide today" list, be honest and cancel or convert it into an async update.

After the meeting, write a three-line summary: Decisions, Owners, Deadlines. Compare how that feels against your usual "we'll remember" approach.

Watch out

Starting meetings with "so, what are we talking about?" because nobody wrote an agenda. Keeping recurring meetings on the calendar out of habit, even when there's nothing specific to discuss. Trying to cram planning, status and big decisions into one shapeless session. And ending without a clear summary, guaranteeing that you'll have the same conversations again in a few weeks.

Topic: .... Date: ....

1:1 Template

Regular 1:1s are one of the most effective tools you have as a producer or lead. They keep people aligned, surface problems early and reduce surprises.
A 1:1 is not a mini status meeting. It's a recurring space where you and one person look at the project and their situation together and decide what needs to change.

What 1:1s are for
A useful 1:1 touches three areas:

- Project: priorities, blockers, quality of work, collaboration.
- Person: workload, motivation, stress, growth.
- You as a lead: what you're doing that helps or gets in the way.

Use 1:1s to ask questions you can't ask in a group: "What's really blocking you?", "What's frustrating in how we work?", "Where are we wasting time?".
Avoid turning them into:

- A read-through of the task tracker.
- A monologue where you talk most of the time.
- A place where feedback appears only when something went very wrong.

A simple 1:1 flow
You don't need a script, just a spine you can return to:

1. **Check-in (5 minutes)**

Genuinely ask: "How are you doing?" Listen for energy level, stress, or anything clearly affecting work.

2. **Work now (10–15 minutes)**

Focus on outcomes, not only tasks. For example: "What went well since we last spoke?", "What's currently blocking you?", "Where are we redoing work unnecessarily?"

3. **Looking ahead (5–10 minutes)**

Align on the next weeks: "Here's what I think your focus should be – does that match your view?", "Is there something you'd like to pick up or hand over?"

4. **Feedback both ways (5 minutes)**

Give one or two concrete pieces of feedback tied to behaviour, not personality. Then ask: "Is there anything I'm doing that makes your work harder?", "What's one thing I could do differently to help you?"

You won't go deep on all four parts every time. The point is to have a consistent structure rather than improvise from zero.

Tiny notes template
For each person, keep a simple 1:1 page with four headings:

- Wins – what went well.
- Issues – problems, blockers, concerns.
- Needs – support, clarity, tools, skills they asked for.
- Actions – what each of you promised to do before the next 1:1.

After the conversation, add 1–3 bullets under each. Start the next 1:1 by checking the previous Actions: "Last time we said we'd do X and Y – did that happen?" This is where trust is either built or damaged.

Cadence that you can keep
For key people, a bi-weekly 1:1 is usually enough; for others, monthly. Rarer than that and you're always in "catch-up mode". If you constantly cancel or move 1:1s, you're sending a clear signal about priority. If you genuinely can't sustain the number of 1:1s you have, reduce the list intentionally – don't pretend they exist.

Try this
On the right-hand page, pick three people you should have regular 1:1s with. For each, write: frequency, one thing you want to understand better about their work, and one thing you suspect they need from you.
Use the flow and notes template for the next two 1:1s, then adjust details – but keep the core idea: a regular, structured conversation focused on both the project and the person.

Watch out
Using 1:1s only when something goes wrong. Letting them slip into rushed status updates. Talking the whole time instead of listening. Asking for honest feedback and then defending yourself against every answer. And promising changes during 1:1s that never show up in how you actually run the project.

Topic: .... Date: ....

Feedback Framework (SBI/COIN)

Feedback is not about "being brutally honest" or "sugar-coating so nobody gets hurt". In a production role, your job is to say hard things in a way that helps people change behaviour without humiliating them. Frameworks like SBI and COIN give you a simple spine, so you don't improvise in the heat of the moment.
This page is about using them in tougher situations: missed expectations, poor collaboration, bad meetings – the stuff that actually happens in gamedev.

SBI – Situation / Behavior / Impact
SBI breaks feedback into three pieces:

- Situation – when/where it happened.
- Behavior – what the person did or said.
- Impact – what it caused (for people, project, player).

Bad top-down feedback in a crunch situation:
"You're unprofessional and people can't rely on you."
That's a label, not feedback. SBI version:
"Situation: During yesterday's build review at 15:00,
Behavior: you joined 20 minutes late and hadn't looked at the latest build notes.
Impact: the team spent time re-explaining known issues, and we couldn't make two key decisions we needed before handoff."
Now the person knows what you're talking about and why it matters. You can then add what you need next time:
"For future reviews, I need you there on time and prepared, because you're the main point of contact for this area."
SBI doesn't make the message soft. It makes it specific and fair.

COIN – Context / Observation / Impact / Next steps
COIN adds one more element: what happens now.

- Context – where this sits in the bigger picture.
- Observation – what you saw/heard.
- Impact – effect on people / project / players.
- Next steps – what you expect to change.

Imagine a recurring communication issue:
Bad version:
"You never communicate, the team is in chaos."
COIN version:
"Context: We're in the last month before content lock, so coordination between design and code is critical.
Observation: In the last two weeks, three times you changed enemy behaviours directly in the data without updating the design channel or the task tracker.
Impact: level designers built encounters on outdated assumptions, QA logged bugs that were actually intentional changes, and we lost a full day re-aligning.
Next steps: From now on, any gameplay change that affects other disciplines needs a short note in the design channel and an updated ticket before you push it. I'll check in at the end of the week to see if this process works for you."
COIN is useful when the behaviour is ongoing and you need an explicit new agreement, not just a "don't do that".

When it gets emotional
Frameworks don't remove emotion, but they stop it from taking over. If you're angry, SBI/COIN force you to slow down: identify the situation, the behaviour and the impact before you speak. Often you realise parts of the story are guesswork – you can then ask instead of accuse. If someone reacts defensively, you can go back to the structure: "Here's the situation I'm talking about; here's what I saw; here's the impact. Is there something I'm missing?" You're arguing about facts and effects, not about whether they're a "good person".

Try this
On the right-hand page, write one piece of feedback you've been avoiding – something important and uncomfortable. First, note the "bad" version you would say if you were tired and impatient. Then rewrite it in SBI and COIN formats.
Compare all three. If you wouldn't want to receive your own "bad" version from a lead, don't send it to anyone else.

Watch out
Using frameworks as a script to dump criticism without empathy. Hiding behind "I'm just giving feedback" when you're actually venting. Staying at the level of vague labels ("unprofessional", "lazy", "genius") instead of behaviours. And forgetting that, after even the best-structured feedback, people mainly watch what you do next – whether your own behaviour and decisions actually match the standards you just described.

Topic: .... Date: ....

Stakeholder Map

On a PC/Steam project (with or without a publisher), "stakeholders" are not just people on slides. They're anyone whose expectations, money or work are strongly affected by your decisions: team, management, publisher, platforms, community, sometimes outsourcers.
If you don't map who really has a say, every bigger decision turns into guessing: "kto się obrazi, jeśli to zmienimy?". This page is about making that landscape visible, so you can plan changes in scope, date and budget like an adult project, not like a surprise party.

Not all stakeholders are equal (and that's fine)
Roughly, you'll see a few recurring groups:

- Core team – designers, programmers, artists, QA, producer. High involvement, often high knowledge, medium formal power.
- Management / founders / investors – high power, low time, strong interest in budget, risk, long-term brand.
- Publisher / business partners – medium–high power depending on contract; care about commercial performance, milestones, positioning.
- Platforms – stores, first parties; power over visibility, approvals, compliance.
- Community / players – low formal power, but huge impact on reputation, sales, and internal morale.
- Freelancers / outsource – low formal power, but they see bottlenecks and misalignment early.

Some of these people have real authority but almost no time. Others (QA, support, community) have lots of insight but little formal say. Your job is not to pretend everyone is equal, but to know who's where and communicate accordingly.

A simple mapping lens: influence and expectation
You don't need a big matrix. On the notes page, think in two dimensions:

1. Influence – how much this group can actually change outcomes (sign off, veto, delay, cut funding, block launches).
2. Expectation – what they care deeply about (quality, date, scope, revenue, reputation).

For example:

- Management: high influence; expect no catastrophic budget/time overrun and a believable path to revenue.
- Publisher: high influence; expect agreed scope by milestones, predictable communication, no PR disasters.
- Core team: medium influence; expect clarity, realistic goals, not being burned out by surprise decisions.
- Community: indirect influence; expect honesty, visible progress after promises, and not being misled.

Once you see this, you can plan: if you move release by three months or cut a whole feature pillar, who must be in the loop, in what order, and with what message?

Using the map for real decisions
Stakeholder mapping matters most when something big shifts: scope cuts, delays, platform changes, model changes, major design pivots.
For each such decision, you can ask:

- Who must be involved in making this call?
- Who must be informed before it goes public?
- Who will be most surprised or hurt if we don't manage expectations?

Then you can tailor communication:

- Management gets a short, honest risk/benefit summary.
- Publisher gets options and impact on roadmap/marketing.
- Team gets context and space to ask "what does this mean for us?".
- Community gets a clear story of what's changing and why, at the right time.

Without this, you end up with random leaks, last-minute panics and broken trust.

Try this
On the right-hand page, draw a simple table with four columns: Group, Influence (High/Med/Low), What they care about, When we must talk to them.
Fill it for at least: core team, management/founders, any publisher/partner, main platform, and players/community.
Then, think of one realistic big decision for your current project (delay, scope cut, platform change) and mark with a star which groups you'd need to handle carefully. That starred row is your first draft playbook for real life.

Watch out
Treating "stakeholder" as synonymous with "who pays the bills" and ignoring QA, support and community until something explodes. Pretending everyone has equal voice when they don't – or worse, pretending nobody has clear authority. Making big calls on scope, date or budget without mapping who will be blindsided. And assuming that silence from powerful stakeholders means consent, when it often just means they weren't actually brought into the conversation.

Topic: .... Date: ....

Decision Log

In most teams, big decisions happen in passing: a late-night call, a hallway chat, a DM thread. A month later nobody remembers who agreed to what, or why. Arguments restart from zero, scope slowly grows back, and people say "but I thought we decided...".

A decision log is just a tiny habit that replaces collective amnesia with a shared memory. It doesn't have to be a system. One page that the core team actually uses is enough.

What a decision log gives you

For a producer or lead, a simple log helps you:

- Reduce re-litigation – you can point to when you agreed to cut X or slip Y.
- Protect the team – when scope, deadlines or budget change, there is a record of why.
- Align stakeholders – everyone sees the same version of events, not their own story.

It also changes how conversations feel. When people know that important decisions will be written down, they push for clarity instead of vague "we'll see".

A very simple format

You don't need more than five fields. On paper or in a lightweight document, create a small table for the core team:

- Date – when the decision was made.
- Topic – short label ("Tutorial scope cut", "Delayed console release").
- Decision – what you actually decided, in one or two sentences.
- Who was involved – names/roles of people in the discussion.
- Why – the key reasons, constraints or data behind it.

Optional: a small "Follow-up" note if there is a clear next step ("communicate to publisher by...", "update roadmap by...").
This is not a transcript. It's a snapshot of the outcome. If it takes longer than a couple of minutes to write, you're overdoing it.

What belongs in the log

You don't need to log every micro-choice. Focus on decisions that:

- Change scope in a visible way (cutting/adding major features, platforms, modes).
- Move dates (launch, big milestones) or change budget / team size.
- Alter business model (pricing, monetisation, platforms) or public promises.

Large design or tech decisions can also belong there if they shape the project for months (engine choice, core loop pivot, "we drop co-op" level changes).

If you hesitate – "is this big enough?" – ask: Will people still argue about this three months from now? If yes, log it.

Keeping it visible

A decision log only works if the core team knows it exists and can see it. Treat it as a shared reference, not your private notebook. When a new big decision is taken, say explicitly: "Let's put this in the decision log."
When conflict appears later – someone wants to bring back a cut feature, or claims a date was "never really agreed" – you can gently point to the entry. The goal is not to win arguments, but to remind everyone what you actually decided with the information you had at the time.

Try this

On the right-hand page, write down the last three major decisions your project made about scope, dates or budget. For each, fill in Date, Topic, Decision, Who was involved, Why.
If this exercise is hard because you're not sure what was decided or who agreed, that's your signal: you don't just need a decision log; you need it now.

Watch out

Letting all important decisions live in private DMs and side conversations. Assuming "everyone remembers" what was agreed. Treating the log as bureaucracy instead of a protection against future chaos. And rewriting history after the fact instead of honestly recording what you decided, with all the imperfect information you had on that day.

Topic: .... Date: ....

Conflict Handling Basics – 3–4 Steps

In any real project, people will clash – especially across disciplines. Design wants one thing, code sees a different reality, art feels squeezed in the middle. As a producer or lead, your job is not to "keep everyone happy". Your job is to keep the project healthy and handle conflict before it poisons collaboration.
You don't need therapy skills. You need a simple, repeatable way to move from "we're stuck and angry" to "we understand the problem and have a next step".

Step 1: Hear each side separately (without judging)
First, get out of the public channel. Heated arguments in group chats or big calls rarely end well.
Talk briefly to each side one-on-one:

- Ask what happened from their point of view.
- Ask what they were trying to achieve.
- Ask what they're worried about now.

Listen for facts, constraints and emotions, not only for who is "right". You're trying to understand:

- What decision or behaviour triggered this?
- What they think the other side is ignoring (scope, quality, tech limits, deadlines, players)?

Don't promise outcomes yet. Your only commitment is: "I want to understand this properly before we decide what to do."
Step 2: Define the real problem together
When you bring people back together, do not restart the debate where it left off.
You start by stating the conflict in neutral terms, for example:
"Design wants variable enemy behaviour to keep players engaged; code says current architecture can't support it within this milestone; art is worried about redoing assets."
Then ask: "Can we agree this is the actual problem we're solving?" If someone disagrees, adjust until there is a shared description.
Your goal is to move from "you are wrong" to "we have a shared problem with conflicting constraints". That shift alone often lowers tension.
Step 3: Re-anchor on project goals and criteria
Conflicts escalate when each side optimises for a different invisible goal. You need to make the higher-level criteria explicit:

- What does success look like for this feature / milestone / project?
- What is non-negotiable (for example: stability, performance budget, release date)?
- What can flex (scope, visual fidelity, complexity, number of variants)?

Say it out loud: "Our priority for this milestone is X; therefore between 'perfect solution in three months' and 'good enough in three weeks', we're closer to the second."
This doesn't magically make people agree, but it gives the decision a shared frame, not three separate private ones.
Step 4: Decide or design a time-boxed experiment
After you have the shared problem and criteria, you move to concrete options. Ask:

- "What are two or three realistic options, given our constraints?"
- "What's the smallest test we can run to see which direction works?"

Then you either:

- Make a decision now (as the owner) and explain it in terms of the criteria, or
- Agree on a short experiment: limited time, clear success criteria, specific next check-in.

Examples:

- "We accept the simpler AI variant for this milestone; we'll revisit smarter behaviours for the update."
- "We give code two days to prototype the approach B; if it doesn't meet performance budget, we lock in option A."

Document the outcome briefly (for example in your decision log) so the same conflict doesn't fully reboot later.

Try this
On the right-hand page, think of a real cross-discipline conflict from your past project. In a few lines, rewrite it using the steps above:

- How would you describe the problem neutrally?
- What project criteria should have guided the choice?
- What decision or experiment would you define now?

You're not rewriting history; you're practising a pattern for the next time it happens.

Watch out
Avoiding conflict until people stop talking to each other. Taking sides too early based on who complains first. Letting arguments play out in public channels with an audience. And leaving discussions without a clear decision or experiment – which guarantees the same fight will come back, louder, right when you can least afford it.

Topic: .... Date: ....

Cross-discipline Handoff

Most production pain doesn't come from "bad people". It comes from work jumping between design, art, code and QA with half the context missing. In a hybrid team, where a lot of collaboration is async, a sloppy handoff can easily cost days of rework.
A handoff is simply the moment when ownership of the next step moves to someone else. This page is about the minimum that has to be clear whenever that happens.

The minimum package for any handoff
Whatever discipline you're handing to, the receiver needs five things:

1. Purpose – what this thing is supposed to achieve for the player or the project.
2. Current state – what's already done and what isn't.
3. Constraints – limits on time, scope, performance, style, tools.
4. Dependencies – what this work relies on and what relies on it.
5. Open questions – what is still undecided or needs feedback.

If any of these are only "in someone's head", expect misunderstandings.

A good handoff can be a short comment in the task, a compact doc, or a quick call plus notes – but it must cover those five points clearly enough that the next person doesn't have to guess.

Hybrid teams: assume nobody is online when you are
In a hybrid or remote setup, handoffs are often async: you move a ticket, write a note, go offline. The other person sees it hours later. Design dropping a one-line task like "Polish combat feel", or code sending QA a build link with "please test", will always backfire.
Before you say "done" and pass something on, ask yourself:

- If they read only this ticket or note, would they know what "good" looks like?
- Would they know what is out of scope, so they don't over-polish the wrong things?
- Would they know who to ask if something is unclear?

If the answer is "no", you haven't finished the handoff yet.

One simple example flow
Imagine a feature going from design to implementation to QA. A minimal, healthy flow might look like this:

- Design → implementation:
- The designer writes a short description of the player experience ("what the player should be able to do and feel"), outlines main rules and edge cases, mentions any relevant references, and notes constraints ("must run on existing input scheme", "no new UI screens"). They also flag known open questions: "we're not sure yet about exact damage numbers, start with a rough pass".
- Implementation → QA:
- The programmer updates the ticket with where the feature lives in the build, how to access it (save, cheat, level), what is expected to work now, and what is intentionally missing or temporary. They list known issues so QA doesn't waste time reporting them again.

QA can now focus on finding new problems and checking behaviour against the intent, not on guessing what the feature was supposed to be.

Nothing here requires a huge document. It requires discipline about passing context, not just files and builds.

Try this
On the right-hand page, pick one feature your team worked on recently. In a few lines, describe how it actually moved between disciplines. Then, underneath, rewrite that path using the five elements of a minimum handoff: purpose, current state, constraints, dependencies, open questions.
Mark one concrete change you can introduce this month to make handoffs less dependent on "you had to be in that meeting".

Watch out
Throwing work over the wall with a one-line task title. Assuming "they know what I mean, we talked about it once". Passing ownership without writing down constraints or known issues. And treating handoffs as a formality, instead of the moment where you either save the next person's time – or set them up to fail.

Topic: .... Date: ....

Hiring / Onboarding Micro-checklist

Hiring is not just "getting more hands". In a small or mid-sized team, every new person changes the system: communication lines, expectations, stress on seniors. As a producer, you might not run full HR, but you do own the question: why are we adding this person, and how will we plug them into the project without wasting months?
This page gives you a minimal checklist for before you hire and for the first days/weeks.

Before you hire: do we really need this role?
Before you post anything, be honest with yourself and the team:

1. **Why this role, why now?**

Write one sentence: "We need a [role] to achieve [specific outcome] in the next [timeframe]."
If you can't fill that, you're not ready to hire.

2. **Definition of success (3–6 months)**

What should be true if this hire is working out? For example:

- "We ship X features per milestone with stable quality."
- "We reduce bug backlog by Y%."
- "We unblock art bottlenecks on environments."

3. **Budget and time cost**

Can you afford not only the salary, but also senior time for onboarding and reviews? If nobody can mentor or review this person, you're buying risk, not capacity.

4. **Shape of the role**

Is this a focused role ("gameplay programmer for combat") or a grab bag ("will do design + scripting + tools + community")? Overstuffed roles are red flags. Narrow it until it's believable for one human.

If you can't answer these points in a half-page note, you're likely hiring "just in case" – which is one of the most expensive mistakes you can make.

First days and weeks: plug into project, not just tools
Once the person joins, your goal is simple: get them productive without throwing them into chaos.
Minimum checklist:

1. **Access and basics (day 1–2)**
   - All required accounts: repo, engine, task tracker, chat, documentation, builds.
   - A short orientation: what the project is, what stage it's in, who does what.
   - One clear point of contact for questions (you, or a delegated mentor).
2. **Context pack (first week)**

For their area, give them:

- Current goals (milestone, features, constraints).
- Key documents (vision, high-level design/art/tech summaries).
- Recent decisions relevant to their work (link decision log where possible).

3. **First tasks**

Start with real, small tasks that touch the real pipeline but are low-risk: bug fixes, small content, polish. They should see how work flows through the team without being given the hardest feature on day three.

4. **Early feedback loops**

Don't wait three months to tell them how they're doing. In the first weeks:

- Short check-ins ("How is the setup?", "What's confusing?").
- Clear feedback on first deliveries: what's good, what needs adjusting.

This costs time, but skipping it costs more. A new hire left to "figure it out" will either underperform or quietly leave.

Try this
On the right-hand page, sketch two micro-checklists:

- Pre-hire: one sentence for "why this role", three bullet points for success after 3–6 months.
- First two weeks: list the concrete things a new person in your most likely hire role needs: access, docs, people, first tasks.

If you can't fill these for a role you're thinking about, pause the hire and clarify the need first.

Watch out
Hiring "because everyone is busy" without a clear outcome. Creating Frankenstein roles nobody can succeed in. Bringing people on board with no access, no context and a huge, vague task. And treating onboarding as an afterthought – then blaming the person for not magically understanding your project's unwritten rules.

Topic: .... Date: ....

Culture & Values in Practice

Every studio has "values" written somewhere. Far fewer have values you can actually see in how people behave, how projects are run and who gets promoted. In a small or mid-sized gamedev team, culture is not a slide deck – it's the sum of hundreds of decisions: who you hire, who you listen to, what you tolerate when things get tough.
This page is about pulling values out of the presentation and into daily production.

Values as decisions, not slogans

Common gamedev-style values sound nice: "focus on players", "ownership", "no crunch", "candour", "playtesting first". They only exist if they show up when it hurts.

- "No crunch" means you cut scope or move dates when reality hits – not that you quietly praise people who stay until 2 a.m.
- "Focus on players" means you adjust roadmap based on real feedback and playtest data – not that you quote reviews only when they confirm your original idea.
- "Ownership" means you let people make decisions in their area and back them up, not that you dump responsibility without giving authority.

As a producer or lead, you communicate values mostly through what you reward, ignore or punish. People watch who gets more interesting tasks, who is listened to in meetings, and who gets away with behaviour that breaks the rules on paper.

Turning values into visible behaviour

Pick a small set of values that really matter for this project (three to five is plenty). For each, define:

- What it looks like in practice in day-to-day production.
- What it does not look like, especially in grey-zone situations.

For example, "playtesting first" in production might mean:

- We schedule regular internal playtests and actually show up.
- When playtest or review feedback clashes with our assumptions, we at least discuss changing something.
- We don't ship big features that nobody has played end-to-end.

"No heroics crunch" might mean:

- We treat repeated overtime as a planning failure, not as heroism.
- Leads don't implicitly reward people for "saving" the build by burning out.
- In post-mortems, we ask "how do we avoid this next time?" instead of "who can we push harder?".

When you write this down, you give everyone a shared language: "If we really believe in X, we should act like this, not like that."

Small rituals that carry big signals

Culture also lives in regular practices – things you do on purpose and keep doing even when busy. A few examples that support healthy values:

- A recurring playtest + debrief where anyone can speak up.
- A short retro after milestones, where both successes and failures are discussed without hunting for a scapegoat.
- A weekly show & tell where different disciplines present work-in-progress, not just "finished" stuff.

These don't have to be big events. The important part is consistency and alignment with what you say you care about. A studio that claims "work–life balance" but schedules mandatory late-night playtests sends a very clear counter-signal.

Try this

On the right-hand page, write down three values you say your team or studio has. For each, add two lines:

- "In practice, this looks like..." – list 2–3 concrete behaviours.
- "It does not look like..." – 2–3 behaviours you'll stop tolerating.

Then choose one simple ritual (for example, monthly retro, regular playtest, shared demo day) that clearly supports at least one of those values and that you can realistically maintain for six months.

Watch out

Treating the culture deck as decoration while rewarding the opposite behaviours. Calling it "no crunch" while quietly promoting those who always sacrifice their evenings. Declaring "candour" and then punishing people who bring bad news early. And starting big culture initiatives you drop after two weeks – teaching everyone that, in this studio, values are just another trend that will be forgotten by the next milestone.

Topic: .... Date: ....

Block G
Personal Workflow & Growth

Topic: .... Date: ....

Daily / Weekly Planning Template

As a producer or lead in a hybrid team, your main resource is not "hours worked". It's attention. You're constantly pulled between meetings, fires, long-term thinking and actual deep work. Without a simple planning routine, your day belongs to whoever pings you the loudest.
This page is a minimalist scaffold for planning week and day so you can steer, not just react.

Weekly: anchor points, not a spreadsheet of wishes
Once a week (15–30 minutes is enough), sketch your week at a high level. Think of three layers:

1. **3–5 weekly priorities**

These are outcomes, not tasks. For example:

- "Lock scope for next milestone."
- "Ship and verify Friday build."
- "Finish feedback round for X feature / team member."

If everything is "top priority", nothing is. Be honest: what would make this week a win, even if nothing else got done?

2. **Fixed blocks**

Put in the non-negotiables: key meetings, reviews, 1:1s, deadlines. This is the hard frame of your week.

3. **Buffers and focus time**

Explicitly leave 20–30% of your time unplanned. That's for surprises, escalations and the fact that estimates are optimistic by default. Then mark 2–3 focus blocks (60–120 minutes) for deep work on your top priorities. Treat them like meetings with yourself.
Your weekly plan should fit on half a page. If it looks like a dense Gantt chart, you're planning a fantasy, not a week.

Daily: three things that actually matter
Each morning (or at the end of the previous day), look at your weekly plan and decide what today is really for.
Keep it minimal:

1. **Top 1–3 outcomes**

Write: "If today only these 1–3 things move forward, the day is still worth it." Keep them connected to your weekly priorities. Examples:

- "Clarify scope and owners for UI revamp."
- "Close open loops on publisher feedback."
- "Prepare agenda + materials for milestone review."

2. **Meetings and touchpoints**

List your meetings and 1:1s for the day. For each important one, add one line: "What do I want out of this meeting?" If the answer is "no idea", either define it now or question the meeting.

3. **Focus block(s) and admin**

Decide when you'll have at least one focus block and what you'll do in it. Also decide when you'll handle low-energy tasks (email, admin, simple approvals) so they don't leak into your whole day.
At the end of the day, quickly check: did my time roughly match my declared priorities? If not, why? That reflection matters more than a perfect plan.

Planning in a noisy, hybrid reality
As a producer/lead, you will never have a clean calendar. People will DM you with "small questions", builds will break, priorities will shift. The point of planning is not to freeze the week. It's to give you a default direction so you can consciously decide what to drop when reality hits.
When new urgent work appears, ask:

- "Which existing priority does this replace?"
- "Can this wait until my next buffer, or must it really pre-empt a focus block?"

If everything always wins against your plan, you don't have a plan – you have a wish list.

Try this
On the right-hand page, draft an "ideal but honest" week: 3–5 weekly priorities, fixed blocks, 2–3 focus blocks, visible buffer. Below that, sketch your template for a single day: top 3 outcomes, meetings with intent, one focus block.
Then use this exactly for one week, without polishing. At the end, mark in a different colour what actually happened. The gap between plan and reality is not failure – it's data for adjusting your next iteration.

Watch out
Stuffing every available slot with work and leaving no buffer for reality. Treating the plan as a rigid contract instead of a compass. Planning only around other people's meetings and never around your own deep work. And abandoning planning entirely after one chaotic day, instead of tweaking the system so it fits the way production really behaves.

Topic: .... Date: ....

Priority Matrix for Dev

In production, everything can feel urgent. Builds are breaking, people are pinging you, someone wants a new slide deck for tomorrow. Without a simple way of ranking work, you either burn out on fires or hide in easy tasks that don't move the project. A priority matrix is just a shared language for "what really matters right now". The classic version is a 2×2 grid: Important vs Not Important and Urgent vs Not Urgent. Here's what that actually means in gamedev for a producer or lead.

Important + Urgent – real fires
These are tasks that both matter to the project's success and are on a tight fuse.
Examples:

- Build blocker that stops the team from working.
- Critical bug before a public demo or certification deadline.
- Last-minute issue from publisher/platform that can delay a campaign or release.

You cannot ignore these. But if your whole week lives here, the project is running you, not the other way around. Your job is to fix today's fires and then ask: "What could we change so this doesn't repeat?"

Important + Not Urgent – where progress actually comes from
These tasks move the project and your team forward, but they don't scream for attention.
Examples:

- Clarifying scope for the next milestone before it explodes.
- Improving your build/release process so "urgent" breaks are rarer.
- 1:1s, feedback, hiring, onboarding, documentation.
- Reviewing data and adjusting roadmap based on real signals.

This quadrant is where real leverage lives. In a busy production, it's also what gets sacrificed first. As a lead, protect time for this and help your team see why it matters.

Not Important + Urgent – noise with a deadline
These feel urgent to someone, but they don't change outcomes much.
Examples:

- Random "can you quickly look at this?" that doesn't connect to current priorities.
- Extra reports that nobody actually uses.
- Meetings you're invited to out of habit, not need.

You don't have to be rude, but you do have to be selective. Ask: "What happens if I say no or 'next week'?" Often, the answer is "nothing". Delegate, batch, or decline as politely as you can.

Not Important + Not Urgent – distractions
These are the comfort tasks: they feel like work but don't matter.
Examples:

- Over-polishing internal docs nobody will read.
- Reorganising boards instead of deciding.
- Diving into details of areas you don't own, just because they're more fun.

They're not evil in small doses, but they should never dominate your time.

Making the matrix a shared tool
This only really pays off if other people use the same logic. When discussing tasks with your team, you can ask:

- "Which quadrant is this in for us this week?"
- "If we say yes to this new request, what drops out of Important + Not Urgent?"

Over time, people start to sort their own work this way and bring you clearer trade-offs instead of raw chaos.

Try this
On the right-hand page, write down 10 things currently on your plate (mix production, dev, communication). Mark each as Important/Not Important and Urgent/Not Urgent, then place them into the four quadrants.
Pick one item from Important + Not Urgent and block time for it this week. Pick one from Not Important + Urgent or Not Important + Not Urgent and consciously drop, delegate, or postpone it.

Watch out
Treating everything as Important + Urgent and living in permanent fire mode. Spending your best energy on tasks that are comfortable but low impact. Using the matrix only in your own head instead of giving the team a shared way to talk about priorities. And pretending you "have no time" for Important + Not Urgent work, while your calendar is full of meetings and tasks that don't really move the game forward.

Topic: .... Date: ....

Deep Work & Focus Blocks in Production

As a producer or lead, your calendar fills itself. Messages, quick questions, meetings, new fires. It's easy to end most days exhausted without being able to point to a single thing you truly moved forward. Deep work is not a luxury for "quiet weeks". It's the time you spend on thinking and decisions that actually change the project.

Deep work here doesn't mean disappearing for days. It means short, protected blocks of focus on work that requires your full brain: designing a realistic milestone, thinking through a scope cut, reviewing data, writing a clear spec, preparing hard feedback, untangling a recurring problem.

Start small: 2–3 honest blocks per week

Don't plan four hours of monk-like silence every day. In production that's a fantasy. Instead, aim for two or three focus blocks per week, 60–90 minutes each, as a starting point.

When you plan your week, pick those blocks first and attach them to specific outcomes, not vague labels. For example: "Thursday 10:00–11:30 – decide tutorial scope and write summary", "Monday 14:00–15:00 – review data + notes for roadmap adjustment". If a block has no clear purpose, it will be the first thing sacrificed.

Managing availability without vanishing

Being a producer/lead also means being reachable. The trick is to make your availability predictable, not constant.

Tell your team something like: "These hours I'm focused and not watching chat unless something is really on fire; these other slots are when I'm available for quick questions." You're not hiding. You're giving a clear contract: there is time for ad hoc help and time for work that keeps the project stable long term.

At the same time, group reactive work into windows. Instead of answering every ping instantly, handle messages, small requests and email in one or two short bursts. The project will not collapse because you replied 45 minutes later instead of 45 seconds.

Inside a focus block

When the block starts, pick one thing and stick with it. No inbox, no "I'll just check Slack quickly". If a new thought pops up ("I should also talk to X about Y"), write it down and come back to the task. The goal of the block is progress, not perfection: getting from 0 to a rough draft or from chaos to a clear decision is a win.

You will sometimes be interrupted. When that happens, pause for two seconds and ask yourself: "Is this a real production fire or just habit?" If it's not a fire, you can say: "I'm in the middle of something, I'll get back to you after X." If it is a fire, you consciously decide to break the block, not slide out of it by default.

Try this

On the right-hand page, sketch next week with two 60–90 minute focus blocks. For each, write exactly what you'll work on and why it matters. At the end of the week, note what actually happened: did you use the blocks, what interrupted them, what you got done. Adjust the timing and number of blocks based on reality, not on guilt.

Watch out

Treating deep work as something you do "if there's time left" – there never is. Booking huge, unrealistic chunks you will always cancel. Disappearing without telling anyone and then being surprised people keep interrupting you. And using focus time to escape into low-impact "busy work" instead of the difficult, important thinking that the rest of the team secretly expects you to do.

Topic: .... Date: ....

My Learning Backlog

As a producer or lead, your "toolset" is not just software and templates. It's skills: how you handle scope, read data, talk to people, negotiate with partners, make calls under uncertainty. Projects come and go, but these skills compound over years. The problem is that in day-to-day production, learning becomes "something I'll think about when things calm down" – which never really happens.

A learning backlog is simply a short, living list of skills you're deliberately levelling up, not a random pile of saved links.

Two horizons: now and the next few years

Think of your learning in two timeframes:

- Skills for now – that help you run your current project better:
- scope management, planning realistic milestones, risk handling, feedback conversations, cross-discipline communication, build/release discipline.
- Skills for the next 2–3 years – that open doors for your career:
- roadmap and portfolio thinking, business and monetisation basics, data/telemetry literacy, negotiations with publishers/platforms, leading other leads.

"Now" skills reduce everyday pain. "Next" skills prevent you from waking up in three years and realising you've only repeated the same year of experience.

A simple structure for your backlog

On your learning backlog page, you don't need a complex system. For each skill, capture four things in one line:

- Skill name – be concrete ("scope cuts conversations", "reading Steam data", "running retros"), not just "communication".
- Why it matters – one sentence tied to your reality: "This would reduce X pain on my project" or "I'll need this to move into role Y".
- How you'll practice – in your actual work: "use this on next milestone planning", "apply in next 3 feedback talks", "shadow lead doing publisher call and take notes".
- Horizon – "now" (next 3–6 months) or "later" (1–3 years).

If a skill doesn't have a clear "why" and "how", it's probably just a nice idea, not a priority.

Learning mainly in the project, not outside of it

Courses, books and talks can help, but the core of your growth will be inside the work you already do.
Examples:

- Want better scope management?
- Turn the next scope cut into a deliberate exercise: prepare options, write down the trade-offs, reflect afterwards on what worked and what didn't.
- Want stronger feedback skills?
- Pick SBI/COIN or another framework and commit to using it in the next three 1:1s where you give hard feedback. After each, write two lines: what landed, what felt awkward.
- Want to understand data and telemetry?
- Start with one real dashboard for your game. Ask someone to walk you through it once, then once a week write down one decision or question that came out of looking at the numbers.

The point is to attach learning to specific upcoming situations, not to vague "someday".

Protecting learning from the "later" trap

If you wait for a perfect free window to work on your learning backlog, it will gather dust. Instead, attach each "now" skill to something already on your calendar: a meeting, a milestone, a decision you know is coming.
You don't need hours. You need small cycles of try → notice → adjust.

Try this

On the right-hand page, split it into two columns: Now (3–6 months) and Next (2–3 years). Under "Now", list 3–5 skills that would clearly reduce pain on your current project. Under "Next", 3–5 that move you toward roles you'd like to have.
For each "Now" skill, write one upcoming situation where you will consciously practice it. After you go through that situation, come back and add a short note about what you learned.

Watch out

Collecting courses, links and conference videos as if that alone made you better. Choosing skills because they sound impressive, not because they change your daily reality. Waiting for a mythical quiet period to start learning. And treating growth as something that "the studio" or "the project" should organise for you, instead of a small, continuous practice you own.

Topic: .... Date: ....

Side Projects & Experiments

For many producers and leads, side projects are where you experiment, learn new tools, and build your own IP. They can keep you motivated when the day job is heavy. They can also quietly turn into a second full-time job, eating sleep, health and relationships – and sometimes creating conflicts with your employer.
The goal is not "side projects yes or no", but side projects on purpose.

Be honest: why this project, why now?
Before you commit, answer three questions in one or two sentences each:

- What is this side project for?
- Learning a new engine, testing a genre, building a portfolio piece, developing your own IP, trying leadership on a small team?
- What does "finished enough" look like?
- A playable prototype, a vertical slice, a pitch deck, a small shipped game, a comic issue – not "I'll work on it forever".
- How much time do you actually have?
- Realistic weekly hours, not fantasy. Include energy, family, health. If your answer requires permanent crunch, the plan is not serious.

If you can't answer these without hand-waving, the project is still at the "daydream" stage. That's fine – just don't treat it like a commitment.

Constraints that protect you from yourself
Set a few simple rules up front:

- Time limit: decide how many hours per week you will spend and when. For example: "two evenings and one weekend block, max". If you constantly steal from sleep, you're already off-track.
- Scope limit: define the smallest coherent version. Every new idea goes to a "later" list, not straight into the build.
- Kill / pause criteria: write down when you will pause or stop: "If after three months I still avoid working on it", "if it starts breaking my main job", "if health/family is suffering".

These constraints are not there to kill your enthusiasm. They're there to stop you from slowly recreating crunch, just with yourself as both victim and manager.

Main job first, side project second
Your main job pays the bills and often gives you the raw material for your skills. If the side project consistently hurts your performance at work, you're burning the bridge that funds your "freedom".
Watch for signs: you're constantly tired, late on commitments, more irritable with your team, avoiding hard problems at work because you "spent your brain" the night before. That's a signal to shrink the side project, not to push harder.
Also, be aware of conflict of interest:

- Don't copy code, tools or assets directly from your job into your side project.
- Don't develop a directly competing game if your contract forbids it.
- If you're unsure, read your contract or ask for clarification before you invest months.

Experiments, not lifetime commitments
Treat side projects as limited experiments, not life-or-death stories:

- "Three months to explore this mechanic and decide if it deserves more."
- "One short game to learn this engine, then decide what's next."

Closing an experiment is not failure if you learned what you came to learn.

Try this
On the right-hand page, pick one side project you'd like to focus on. Write:

- Purpose (learning / IP / portfolio – be specific).
- "Finished enough" definition.
- Weekly time budget and when you'll work.
- One or two clear kill/pause criteria.

Look at it as if it was someone else's plan. Would you, as a producer, sign off on this?

Watch out
Running a hidden second job at night and calling it "passion". Using side projects to avoid hard conversations or decisions in your main role. Ignoring contracts and NDAs because "it's just for me". And refusing to pause or kill a side project even when it clearly drains you more than it gives – turning a source of growth into yet another source of guilt.

Topic: .... Date: ....

Career Map (Producer / Designer) – Paths Ahead

Careers in gamedev are rarely straight lines. Studios change, projects die, roles blend. As a producer or designer you can drift from title to title, or you can occasionally stop and ask: where am I, what paths are actually in front of me, and what do I want to bet on?

This page is not about predicting the future. It's about drawing a simple map so you're not just reacting to the next offer.

First: take a clear snapshot of "now"

Before you think about paths, define your current position:

- What is your actual role today – not just title, but what you spend most of your time on?
- On a typical week, how much of your energy goes into production (planning, sync, risk, stakeholders) vs design (systems, content, balancing, UX, narrative)?
- In which type of environment are you working: indie, AA/AAA, service game, single-player premium?

Write it down honestly. "Mid-level designer doing a lot of live-ops planning" or "producer who still designs systems on the side" is more useful than "Game Designer" or "Producer" as a label.

Three common paths for producers and designers

From here, most careers branch along a few recurring directions. None is "better"; each has trade-offs.

1. Deep craft specialist
    - Designer: systems / combat / economy / level specialist, highly hands-on.
    - Producer: live-ops producer, analytics-focused, platform specialist.
    - Pros: strong expertise, clear value on complex projects.
    - Cons: more depth, less say in broad studio direction; risk of being stuck if the narrow niche shrinks.
2. Broad generalist / cross-discipline lead
    - Hybrid producer-designer, product owner, game lead on smaller teams.
    - Pros: you see the whole picture, connect design, tech, art, business; good fit for indie or small studios.
    - Cons: constant context-switching, easier to burn out, and you must be okay with "good enough" in many areas.
3. Leadership / management track
    - Design lead, game director, production director, head of product.
    - Pros: larger influence on projects and teams, decisions that shape whole portfolios.
    - Cons: much less hands-on creation, more people issues and politics; success measured in team outcomes, not your own features.

A fourth option is changing lanes: designer sliding into production, producer moving toward more creative direction. This can make sense if your current role already leans that way – but it should be a conscious choice, not just "the studio needed someone".

Mapping your possible futures

On your map, you don't need ten options. Pick two or three roles you could realistically see yourself in 3–5 years from now. For each, ask:

- In what kind of studio would this role make sense for me (size, projects, culture)?
- What do people in that role actually do all week? (Not what the title suggests.)
- Which skills, behaviours and experiences seem consistently needed there?

Compare that list with your current "snapshot". The gaps you see are not reasons to give up; they are clues. Maybe you need more experience shipping live content, more practice managing people, or more time designing and iterating on one specific type of system instead of "a bit of everything".

Try this

On the right-hand page, draw three boxes:

- Left: "Where I am now" – role, main activities, environment.
- Middle and right: two roles you might want in 3–5 years (title + type of studio).

Under each future role, write three skills or experiences you believe are essential there. Put a star next to any that you can start developing inside your current project.

Watch out

Letting your whole career be defined by which project happens to need you next. Chasing titles without understanding what the day-to-day really looks like. Saying you want leadership while refusing to let go of being the main individual contributor. And telling yourself "I'll think about my path later" until you realise you've repeated the same year of experience five times instead of growing through five different years.

Topic: .... Date: ....

Burnout Early Warning Signs

Burnout rarely arrives overnight. In production it often creeps in slowly: one more milestone, one more "just this weekend", one more fire. As a producer or lead, you're good at pushing through for the team – which also makes you good at ignoring your own warning signals.

This page is about noticing early signs in yourself, not diagnosing anyone else. It's also not medical advice. If you're worried about your health or functioning, talking to a doctor or mental health professional is the right move, not a failure.

Four clusters of early signals

Everyone is different, but burnout often shows up in four overlapping areas. You don't need all of them for something to be wrong.

Emotional

- You feel unusually irritated by normal problems ("this again? I'm done").
- You drift into cynicism: default reaction to new ideas is eye-rolling.
- You care less and less about outcomes you used to be invested in.

Cognitive

- It's harder to focus for more than a few minutes.
- Simple decisions feel heavy, you keep postponing them.
- You read the same message or spec three times and still don't absorb it.

Physical

- Sleep is off: can't fall asleep, wake up too early, or wake up tired.
- Headaches, tension, stomach issues show up more often.
- You live on caffeine and sugar just to feel "normal".

Behavioural

- You procrastinate more, especially on important tasks.
- You avoid messages, meetings or people that "need something from you".
- You disconnect from hobbies and people outside work because you're "too tired".

Any single symptom might come from something else (illness, life events), which is exactly why self-diagnosing from a checklist isn't enough. But if several of these stay with you for weeks and your lifestyle hasn't changed dramatically, treat that as a serious signal – not "just how gamedev is".

The crunch trap: when abnormal becomes "normal"

Chronic overtime, constant "saving the build", being the person who always picks up dropped balls – all of that is often praised in the short term. Over time it trains you to ignore your own limits.

If you catch yourself thinking "this is unsustainable, but I'll handle it a bit longer" for the third or fourth time, that's not resilience. That's you burning future capacity.

As a producer/lead you might also be complicit: you tell yourself "I'm protecting the team, I'll absorb the pain". That sometimes works for a crisis; it doesn't work as a lifestyle.

First responses you actually control

You can't fix everything alone, but you do have levers. Typical first steps:

- Name it clearly – even just on paper: "I'm more irritable, tired, and unfocused than usual for the last X weeks."
- Adjust load where you can – push back on non-essential work, renegotiate deadlines, stop volunteering for every extra task.
- Talk to someone you trust – a peer, mentor, manager; "I'm not okay and I need to adjust a few things" is a valid sentence.
- Check your basics – sleep, food, movement, time off. They won't solve everything, but without them nothing else works.

If symptoms are strong, last a long time, or you're worried about depression, anxiety, health issues: see a professional (doctor, psychologist, psychiatrist). Many burnout-like symptoms overlap with other conditions; guessing alone is risky.

If you ever feel close to harming yourself or completely losing control, that's emergency territory – reach out to local emergency services or crisis support lines immediately.

Try this

On the right-hand page, mark which emotional, cognitive, physical and behavioural signs you've noticed in yourself in the last month. Next to each, write one small action you can take in the next two weeks (a boundary, a conversation, a check-up, a change in schedule).

You're not weak for needing this. You're doing the same thing you'd do for a project: noticing risk early and acting before it turns into a full-blown disaster.

Topic: .... Date: ....

Boundaries & “No” Checklist

As a producer or lead, you’re the buffer between people who want more (management, publisher, platforms) and people who are already at their limit (your team, including you). If you never say “no” or “not like this”, the cost doesn’t vanish – it just lands on health, quality and trust.

This page is about your personal boundaries. Not theoretical ones – the lines past which the job stops being sustainable or acceptable for you.

Time & crunch – where is your line?
Some weeks will be heavier than others. The problem is when “exception” quietly becomes normal.
Ask yourself:

- How many evenings/weekends am I really willing to sacrifice on a regular basis?
- How often do I tell myself “just this milestone” – and how long has that been true?
- If someone looked only at my calendar, czy widziałby „no crunch”, czy stałe nadgodziny?
- What is my non-negotiable minimum for sleep, days off, holidays?

If your honest answers and your actual behaviour don’t match, you’re already crossing your own line – even if nobody explicitly asked you to.

Responsibility & role creep – what is not yours?
In small teams you will wear multiple hats. That’s fine until “helping out” becomes “doing three roles for the price of one”.
Ask:

- Which responsibilities are truly mine to own as producer/lead – and which only landed on me because “someone had to”?
- Am I consistently doing work that should belong to someone else’s role or level?
- If I disappeared for a month, which tasks would actually need a replacement, and which would the team simply drop?

You don’t have to refuse every extra task. But you should be clear when a “temporary favour” is turning into a silent expectation. Boundaries here often sound like: “I can cover this for the next X weeks; after that we need a proper owner or a different plan.”

Communication & behaviour – what is never okay?
Stressful projects can bring out the worst in people: sarcasm, blame, shouting, public shaming. You can’t control everyone, but you can decide what you consider acceptable.
Ask:

- What kinds of comments or behaviours make me think “if this becomes normal here, I don’t want to stay”?
- Have I started treating raised voices, insults, or passive-aggressive digs as “just how X is”?
- When was the last time I calmly said: “This way of talking is not okay for me”?

You don’t need dramatic confrontations. Sometimes boundaries are quiet and firm: you stop laughing at “jokes” that punch down, you don’t join in public pile-ons, you move sensitive conversations to private and keep them respectful.

A small “no” checklist
On the right-hand page, list five things you are not willing to accept in future projects (for example: permanent unpaid crunch, being the only one who communicates bad news, public humiliation, doing two roles indefinitely).
Next to each, write one question you’ll ask yourself when it appears, such as:

- “If I say yes to this again, what am I saying no to?”
- “Would I want my team to accept this as normal?”
- “What would I advise a friend in my situation to do?”

Watch out
Telling yourself “it’s just for now” for months or years. Treating every ask from above as a command, and every complaint from below as your personal failure. Accepting behaviour that would make you tell any junior “you should leave that place” – while staying in it yourself. And forgetting that your “yes” has value only if, from time to time, you are willing to calmly say “no” or “not like this”.

Topic: .... Date: ....

End-of-Project Reflection Template

When a project ends, the instinct is to move on fast: new brief, new fire, new excitement. As a producer or lead, you also carry a lot of invisible baggage from what just happened: decisions, mistakes, half-finished conversations. A short personal reflection is how you turn that chaos into experience you can actually reuse, instead of repeating the same year five times. This is not a team retrospective. This is you+notebook, and an honest look at what you did, what happened, and what you want to do differently next time.

Step 1: Snapshot – what actually happened?
Start with a neutral snapshot, not judgement.
In a few lines each, write:

- The project: what it was (scope, platform, business model), how long it ran, what stage it reached (shipped, cancelled, pivoted, parked).
- Key outcomes: schedule (on time / slips and why), budget (roughly on / off), quality (bugs, reviews, stability), and any business results you know (launch, wishlists, revenue, player reception).

You're not writing a report for management. You're giving your future self enough context so that in two years you still remember what this project actually was.

Step 2: My role – what I really did
Now zoom in on your part of the story. Use three short sections:

- What I actually spent my time on
- Not your title, but reality: "mostly planning and sync", "lots of firefighting builds", "heavy on external partners", "ended up quasi-design lead".
- Three things I did that helped
- Specific actions or habits that clearly improved outcomes or reduced pain for the team.
- Three things I did that hurt or were missing
- Decisions you delayed too long, conversations you avoided, areas where you over-controlled or under-owned.

Write plainly. This isn't for HR. It's for pattern-spotting.

Step 3: Lessons – what I want to keep and change
Turn the story into a few concrete lessons.
You can use prompts like:

- "Next time, I want to do more of..." (e.g. earlier scope cuts, clearer stakeholder mapping, regular decision log updates).
- "Next time, I want to do less of..." (e.g. last-minute changes, agreeing to impossible dates, being the single point of failure).
- "I learned that I tend to..." (e.g. avoid conflict, underestimate testing, overpromise to partners, forget my own limits).

Then choose one or two simple rules for future projects, phrased as "When X, I will Y". For example: "When we move a date, I will immediately write down why and who agreed" or "When I spot crunch creeping in, I will call it out within a week, not after the milestone."

Step 4: Close the loop
Finally, allow yourself a short emotional check:

- What am I proud of, despite everything?
- What do I still regret or feel sore about?
- Is there any conversation I still need to have (or write down for myself) to really close this?

You don't have to fix everything now. The point is to avoid dragging unresolved weight into the next project without even naming it.

Try this
On the right-hand page, follow the four steps with your last finished project. Keep it to one page. If it feels heavy, that's normal. Put the date at the top.
In a future project, when you hit a similar situation, come back and skim this page. Your past self will often have better advice than a random blog post.

Watch out
Turning this into self-punishment instead of learning. Writing only about what the studio or others did wrong, and never about your own part. Skipping the hard parts ("what I avoided, what I regret") because "there's no time". And jumping straight into the next project without ever giving yourself ten honest minutes to turn pain and chaos into something you can actually use.

Topic: .... Date: ....

Year In Review

A year in gamedev can feel like three compressed into one: milestones, launches, cancellations, reorgs, new roles. If you don't stop to look back, everything blurs into "busy". This page is a simple way for you, as a producer or lead, to capture what actually happened – and whether the direction you're moving in still makes sense for you. You're not writing this for HR or LinkedIn. It's a private snapshot: projects, decisions, growth, and how it all felt from the inside.

Projects & key moments – what filled the year?
Start with a neutral inventory, no judgement.
In a few bullets, write:

- Projects you touched: shipped, cancelled, pivoted, parked.
- Key moments: big milestones, launches, crunch stretches, major changes (new role, new studio, new platform, first time leading X).

Then, for each major project, add one line:

- "This project was mostly about..." (learning what? dealing with what kind of chaos? taking on which new responsibility?)

You're giving your future self a timeline so "that crazy year" becomes something you can actually remember and compare.

My work this year – what I actually did
Now focus on your own actions and growth.
Use three short sections:

- What I spent most of my energy on
- Examples: "keeping stakeholders aligned", "unblocking cross-discipline issues", "holding live-ops together", "acting as unofficial design lead".
- Three things I did well
- Situations where your behaviour clearly helped – a decision you made early, a conflict you handled, a process you improved, a person you supported.
- Three things I'd do differently
- Not just "mistakes", but patterns: where you stayed silent too long, overcommitted, avoided tough calls, or ignored your own limits.

Keep it specific: "I handled X publisher escalation calmly and early" is more useful than "I improved communication".

Health, energy, and trade-offs
Work doesn't happen in a vacuum. Without turning this into a diary, do a quick check-in:

- When in the year did I feel most engaged and alive in my work? What was I doing, and in what conditions?
- When did I feel most drained or close to burning out? What was different?
- What did I trade away to get through this year (sleep, hobbies, relationships, focus) – and was it worth it?

You're not looking for perfect balance. You're checking whether the cost of your current way of working is something you're willing to keep paying.

Direction check – is this still my path?
Step back and ask:

- If I had to describe this year in one sentence like a chapter title, what would it be?
- If the next three years looked exactly like this one, would I be okay with that? Why or why not?
- What kind of producer/lead am I slowly becoming, judging by my choices this year?

You don't need a detailed plan for the next year here. Just a sense of whether to continue roughly in this direction, or whether something needs to bend.

Try this
On the right-hand page, follow the four sections:

1. Projects & key moments.
2. My work this year (energy, wins, "do differently").
3. Health and trade-offs.
4. Direction check.

Give yourself 30–60 minutes, max one page. Date it. You can come back to it next year and see not just what changed in your CV, but what changed in you.

Watch out
Reducing the entire year to one launch, one failure, or one bad month. Writing only about what others did to you and never about what you chose. Using this as a stick to beat yourself with instead of a way to see patterns. And rushing straight into the next year's goals without even pausing long enough to ask: "Is this still the game I want to be playing?"

Topic: .... Date: ....

Notes / Free Space

Every tool in this notebook was born out of very specific contexts: my own projects, the constraints I was under, the data I could and couldn't see, the feedback I received, the advice people gave me, and the mistakes I made trying to keep games on track. This last pair of pages is where your experience starts to bend that system to your reality. It's not a bonus area – it's where you stop only borrowing other people's templates and begin shaping your own.

You're not obliged to keep this space tidy. Think of it as a small lab attached to your office: Post-its on the wall, half-baked ideas, things you're trying out for a few weeks to see if they stick.

Your workflow will never look like anyone else's
Even if two people have the same title, their day looks different: different studios, teams, expectations, pain points. That's why no single template – including the ones in this book – will fit perfectly.
This space is where you can:

- Bend or remix tools from earlier sections so they fit your reality.
- Capture patterns you notice in your own projects that no generic framework ever mentions.
- Sketch small systems that only make sense to you, but make your work easier.

You might design your own version of a decision log, a variant of the 30/60/90 plan that matches your release cadence, or a personal shorthand for stakeholder maps. It doesn't have to be pretty. It has to be honest and useful.

Use it as a running scratchpad, not a monument
Instead of trying to create a "perfect" system here, treat these pages as work-in-progress:

- When you find yourself repeating the same calculation, thought process or checklist in your head, move it here.
- When you test a new ritual (weekly review, meeting format, feedback questions), jot down how you're doing it and what you're observing.
- When you get advice from someone you respect – a mentor, senior, peer – capture the parts that actually resonate with you, not the whole speech.

Some of what you write will become part of your standard kit. Some will turn out to be dead ends. That's normal. Labs have failed experiments on the shelves.

Breaking the "rules" is part of the point
Every previous page gave you a specific pattern: context, a mini-framework, a "Try this", a "Watch out". Here you're allowed to break that pattern completely.
You can mix languages. You can sketch. You can write messy lists or half-sentences only you understand. You can paste in a tiny printed diagram, then scribble over it. The test is simple: when you open these pages in the middle of a stressful week, do they help you think more clearly?
If a tool from earlier in the notebook doesn't quite fit, clone it here and hack it until it does: remove steps, merge sections, add prompts that address problems you see in your studio but never on slides.

Try this
On the right-hand page, start with one thing that has been living only in your head: a small checklist you always run before releases, a way you prepare for hard 1:1s, a pattern you see in your own mistakes. Write it down in any format that feels natural.
Then, over the next few weeks, notice when you actually use it. Add short notes about what worked, what didn't, and what you want to change. Let these pages evolve with you, instead of trying to finish them in one sitting.

Watch out
Treating every external framework as sacred while never giving yourself permission to adapt it. Leaving this space blank because you're waiting for a "perfect" idea. And assuming that your way of working should look exactly like someone else's, instead of gradually building a toolkit that matches the kind of producer or lead you are actually becoming.

Topic: .... Date: ....

Topic: .... Date: ....

Topic: .... Date: ....

Table of Content

Topic: .... Date: ....

Table of Content

Topic: .... Date: ....

Afterword

This workbook started as something much smaller and much more selfish.
I wanted a notebook with reminders on the left page and space for my own chaos on the right. I usually write on the right side, and I needed a quiet voice on the left: "Hey, remember this. Don't repeat that mistake again. Check this before you say yes."

The more I sketched, the more I felt it could be useful for more than just one producer who likes to write on the right side of the page. It could be a set of pages you can bend to your own reality – whether you're just entering gamedev or you've been here long enough to know how easy it is to lose the big picture.
I came into games because playing and modding stopped being enough. I wanted to make things, not just consume them. Over time, "wannabe designer" slowly turned into "the person responsible for teams and projects". The titles changed, the scale of projects changed, but two things stayed the same: I still like games, and I still care about the people trying to build them under very imperfect conditions.
A lot of what's in these pages comes from less-than-perfect conditions.

There were years when impostor syndrome was a constant background process: the feeling that the challenges were too big, that I didn't really know what I was doing, that one day someone would notice I'm just stitching things together as I go. On top of that, there was the "superhero mode": the belief that I had to deliver at any cost, never admit I didn't know something, never show doubt – because that would be "unprofessional" or shameful.

Combine that with the usual fears: that someone will say I'm doing it wrong, that there are faster and smarter ways I never learned, that my gaps in knowledge will finally be exposed. It's not a great mix. Even if, on paper, everything looks fine, carrying all of this can be exhausting.
I've had time to work through most of that. I don't write this from the bottom of the hole. But I remember very well what it feels like to operate with all of that sitting on your shoulders.

If any of this sounds familiar, I want you to hear three simple things clearly:
Never be afraid to ask, to say "I don't know", or to ask for help.
You are surrounded by people who want you and the project to succeed. Many of them are more than willing to explain, share tricks, or say "yeah, this is hard for everyone". Not using that support doesn't make you stronger – it just makes the job heavier.
Don't lie.
It's tempting to cover a mistake, hide a delay, pretend you've already done something, or that you understand when you don't. That path always leads to more complex lies and more pressure. The cost of cleaning up after a small honest problem is almost always lower than cleaning up after a long-running fiction.
Don't erase your own contribution.
When something goes wrong, we're quick to take responsibility. When something goes well, it's easy to say "it was nothing" or "anyone could have done it". If you did good work, acknowledge it to yourself and let others see it too. You're not stealing credit; you're recognising reality.

Everything in this workbook is a snapshot of my experience in a very specific time and space: particular projects, teams, platforms, markets, pieces of data I had (or didn't have), advice I received, and mistakes I made in both good and bad moments. None of it is "the one true way". It's just one long, structured attempt to make the next project a little less chaotic than the last one.

My hope is simple: that some of these pages make your work a bit easier, your decisions a bit clearer, and your load a bit lighter – and that from here, you take what's useful, ignore what isn't, and slowly build your own set of tools on top of it.

If that happens, this workbook did its job.

Have fun and play some games!
Leszek

www.ingramcontent.com/pod-product-compliance
Ingram Content Group UK Ltd.
Pitfield, Milton Keynes, MK11 3LW, UK
UKHW060224061026
15625UKWH00008B/487

9 788397 628120